Building a Resilient SAP Enterprise

Build a resilient SAP enterprise in the era of RISE, GROW, and cloud-native services

Soulat Khan

Sunny Patwari

Ganesh Suryanarayanan

bpb

www.bpbonline.com

First Edition 2025

Copyright © BPB Publications, India

ISBN: 978-93-65895-490

To View Complete
BPB Publications Catalogue
Scan the QR Code:

www.bpbonline.com

Dedicated to

Our families for their patience,
our mentors for their encouragement,
and our friends for challenging us

About the Authors

- **Soulat Khan** is currently working as the worldwide leader for SAP solution architecture for customers, and partners and managed the technical alliance for SAP at **Amazon Web Services** (**AWS**). Soulat is a recognized expert in SAP cloud transformations having spoken at Americas SAP user group conferences, AWS re:Invent, and numerous industry events. With over 20 years of enterprise technology experience, he specializes in helping organizations modernize their SAP landscapes and build resilient cloud architectures. This book reflects his practical experience and strategic insights in building future-ready SAP enterprises, combining deep technical knowledge with business-focused outcomes.

- **Sunny Patwari** is an SAP leader at Amazon Web Services (AWS), specializing in FinTech and currently overseeing SAP implementations for AWS Infrastructure Finance and Supply Chain. Previously, he led the Worldwide Strategic Alliance for SAP at AWS and served as a subject matter expert for RISE with SAP and Business Technology Platform. With deep expertise in architecting and delivering complex, global SAP transformations, Sunny has supported organizations across a wide range of industries, including semiconductors, pharmaceuticals, aerospace, and defense. He has worked closely with customers in diverse market segments to accelerate their cloud migrations using RISE with SAP and Cloud native services.

- **Ganesh Suryanarayanan** serves as a Principal SAP Innovation Architect at AWS, where he crafts sophisticated ERP solutions for global enterprises. His unique ability to harmonize SAP processes with AWS capabilities helps organizations achieve their digital transformation goals while optimizing both performance and cost. This book reflects his practical experience and strategic insights in building future-ready SAP enterprises, combining deep technical knowledge with business-focused outcomes.

About the Reviewers

❖ **Sriharsha Narasimhan** is a strategic leader, board director, and certified independent director with over 37 years of global experience in digital technologies, corporate governance, digital transformation, risk, and cybersecurity. He is an expert in aligning technology strategies with regulatory mandates and advises C-level executives of financial institutions. Sriharsha has a proven track record in implementing mission-critical infrastructure projects that deliver operational resiliency and foster innovation through collaboration.

As the former CTO for Mission Critical Solutions and Aruba Networks at Hewlett-Packard Enterprise, Sriharsha collaborated closely with C-suite executives and ecosystem partners to formulate and execute holistic strategies aligned with the business vision and objectives. He has extensive experience in building scalable, secure, and operationally resilient solutions for HPE's infrastructure offerings, particularly for SAP ECC and SAP HANA requirements. Notably, for the BFSI vertical, he has architected mission-critical and highly scalable infrastructure for debit card/digital payments and core banking systems. Additionally, Sriharsha has developed competencies in automation, digital experiences, AIOps, cybersecurity, IT/OT integration, and IoT. In his spare time, he reads fictional, comics, and technical books and listens to international music.

❖ **Jeyaganesh Viswanathan** is a seasoned SAP Solution Architect with over 20 years of extensive experience in implementing and managing complex SAP environments. Currently serving as IT Lead at Zoetis Pharmaceutical, he architects enterprise-wide SAP with deep integration experience across SAP Products.

As a certified SAP professional, Jey has led transformative projects for industry giants, including L'Oréal, Apple, BASF, and Wolters Kluwer, orchestrating SAP implementations across 45+ countries.

A published author with SAP PRESS, Jey has written on SAP ACTIVATE methodology and contributed research papers to peer-reviewed journals focusing on AI, Robotic Process Automation, and SAP advanced variant configuration systems. His ability to bridge theoretical concepts with practical implementation has established him as a thought leader in the SAP community. Throughout his career, Jey has demonstrated exceptional leadership in managing cross-functional teams and driving innovation, consistently delivering results that align with organizational objectives.

Acknowledgements

This book is a labor of love, a testament to the passion we hold for our work and the cherished relationships we have built with partners, customers, and colleagues throughout our years in the SAP ecosystem. Every page reflects countless conversations, shared challenges, and collective victories that have shaped our understanding of enterprise transformation.

First and foremost, we extend our deepest gratitude to our families. Their understanding during the long hours, their unwavering support through missed dinners and working weekends, and their constant encouragement as we documented our experiences have been the foundation of this endeavor. Their love has been our anchor throughout this journey.

At its core, this book is about building a resilient SAP enterprise, a vision that would not be possible without acknowledging SAP itself, a pioneering force that continues to transform business processes globally. For nearly five decades, SAP has not just developed software; it has revolutionized how organizations operate, adapt, and thrive in an ever-evolving business landscape.

To our customers and partners: your trust in allowing us to be part of your transformation journey has been our greatest privilege. Every challenge you have shared, every success we have celebrated together, and every lesson we have learned collectively has contributed to the insights within these pages. Your willingness to let us guide you through complex transformations has enriched our perspective, and we're honored to share these experiences with a broader audience.

We are profoundly grateful to BPB Publications for their exceptional guidance and expertise. Their unwavering support transformed our vision into reality, helping us navigate the intricacies of the publishing process with precision and care. Their commitment to excellence mirrors the high standards we strive for in our professional endeavors.

Special appreciation goes to our reviewers, technical experts, and editors whose meticulous attention to detail and insightful feedback have elevated this manuscript. Their expertise has helped ensure that our practical experience translates into actionable knowledge for our readers.

This book represents not just our knowledge, but the collective wisdom of a community dedicated to excellence in enterprise transformation. Together, we continue to build more resilient, efficient, and successful businesses through the power of SAP.

Preface

The landscape of SAP development and implementation is undergoing its most significant transformation since the introduction of ABAP in the 1980s. As we navigate this pivotal shift toward cloud-native solutions and software-as-a-service offerings, SAP professionals face both exciting opportunities and complex challenges. This book serves as your comprehensive guide through this evolution, particularly in the era of RISE with SAP, where traditional customization approaches are giving way to new paradigms of solution building. Drawing from extensive experience in enterprise SAP implementations, we have witnessed firsthand the journey from traditional ABAP development to today's cloud-based, full-stack solutions. The emergence of SAP Build, combined with generative AI capabilities and the SAP **Business Technology Platform** (BTP), has created unprecedented possibilities for innovation, while simultaneously introducing new complexities in architecture, security, and deployment.

A central theme of this transformation is the strategic integration between SAP and hyperscaler environments like AWS. Throughout this book, we present practical use cases demonstrating how this powerful combination enables organizations to leverage both SAP's business process expertise and the advanced cloud services of hyperscalers. From data federation and machine learning to serverless architectures and edge computing, we explore how these integration patterns solve real business challenges while maintaining security and governance.

This book bridges the critical gap between traditional SAP development and modern cloud-based approaches. We have structured it to provide both theoretical understanding and practical guidance, ensuring you can confidently navigate SAP's new builder space while maintaining the resilience and reliability your enterprise demands. Each chapter includes concrete use cases drawn from real-world implementations, helping you translate concepts into actionable solutions for your specific business needs.

Whether you are an ABAP developer transitioning to cloud solutions, an integration architect exploring new possibilities, or a DevSecOps specialist seeking to optimize SAP implementations, you will find actionable insights for building and maintaining robust SAP environments. We pay particular attention to the guardrails and best practices necessary for success in this new landscape, while never losing sight of the ultimate goal: delivering business value through well-architected solutions.

As SAP continues its cloud transformation journey, understanding how to leverage these new tools and platforms becomes not just advantageous but essential. This book is your roadmap to mastering this evolving ecosystem, ensuring your SAP enterprise remains resilient, adaptable, and future-ready.

Welcome to the next generation of SAP solution building.

Chapter 1: Introduction to the Modern SAP Enterprise – This foundational chapter sets the stage for modern SAP development, introducing the critical concept of clean core methodology and its impact on business operations. Readers will discover how the evolution from traditional development to API-based applications fundamentally changes the SAP landscape. The chapter explains why maintaining a clean core reduces operational costs and simplifies upgrades while optimizing performance. It addresses the urgent need for ABAP developers and architects to modernize their skill sets, providing a clear pathway to understanding modern SAP development practices alongside the latest available tools and training resources.

Chapter 2: Overview of SAP's Latest Offers, RISE and GROW – A comprehensive exploration of SAP's transformation from perpetual licensing to subscription-based models through RISE and GROW with SAP. The chapter examines how this strategic shift impacts development methodologies, tools, and approaches. Readers will gain clear insights into the differences between traditional S/4HANA development environments and new cloud-based platforms. Special attention is given to the changing landscape of development capabilities, including both new opportunities and limitations in code deployment, configuration management, and change control processes.

Chapter 3: SAP Business Technology Platform and Cloud Provider Integration– An in-depth examination of SAP **Business Technology Platform (BTP)** and its strategic integration with hyperscaler environments. The chapter explores how this powerful combination enables organizations to build scalable, resilient applications while leveraging cloud-native services. Readers will understand the core components of SAP BTP, key integration patterns with hyperscalers like AWS, and practical implementation approaches. The discussion includes real-world examples demonstrating how data federation, API management, and machine learning capabilities create new opportunities for digital transformation and innovation in SAP landscapes.

Chapter 4: Introduction to Generative AI – An exploration of how generative AI is revolutionizing the SAP ecosystem, providing unprecedented capabilities for content creation, process automation, and decision support. The chapter presents SAP's comprehensive approach to business AI, examining the Generative AI Hub and integration patterns with foundation models. Readers will gain practical insights into implementing generative AI solutions within their SAP landscape, understanding key concepts like prompt engineering, RAG, and embeddings. Special focus is given to enterprise use cases and how organizations can balance innovation with security and governance requirements.

Chapter 5: Building Well-Architected Applications on SAP BTP– A detailed guide to applying well-architected principles when developing applications on SAP BTP. The chapter examines the five foundational pillars: operational excellence, security, reliability, performance efficiency, and cost optimization. Readers will learn practical methodologies for evaluating and implementing architectural decisions that maintain resilience while enabling innovation. The discussion includes architectural patterns, implementation strategies, and measurement frameworks that help organizations build SAP applications that are both technically sound and aligned with business objectives.

Chapter 6: Managing Application Security and Costs – A comprehensive examination of security frameworks and cost optimization strategies for SAP cloud deployments. The chapter details the shared responsibility model and its implications for enterprise applications. Readers will understand how to implement effective security controls across their SAP landscape while maintaining operational efficiency. Special attention is given to RISE with SAP security considerations, connectivity options, and practical approaches to cost management. The chapter provides actionable guidance for balancing security requirements with budget constraints in today's complex threat landscape

Chapter 7: Concluding Remarks and Addition Resources– The final chapter synthesizes the book's key concepts into actionable insights for building resilient SAP architectures. It provides a strategic framework for establishing and scaling SAP build environments, with particular attention to future-proofing investments. The chapter serves as both a summary and a roadmap, helping readers plan their next steps in modernizing their SAP development practices.

Coloured Images

Please follow the link to download the
Coloured Images of the book:

https://rebrand.ly/09kfxml

We have code bundles from our rich catalogue of books and videos available at **https://github.com/bpbpublications**. Check them out!

Errata

We take immense pride in our work at BPB Publications and follow best practices to ensure the accuracy of our content to provide with an indulging reading experience to our subscribers. Our readers are our mirrors, and we use their inputs to reflect and improve upon human errors, if any, that may have occurred during the publishing processes involved. To let us maintain the quality and help us reach out to any readers who might be having difficulties due to any unforeseen errors, please write to us at :

errata@bpbonline.com

Your support, suggestions and feedbacks are highly appreciated by the BPB Publications' Family.

Did you know that BPB offers eBook versions of every book published, with PDF and ePub files available? You can upgrade to the eBook version at www.bpbonline.com and as a print book customer, you are entitled to a discount on the eBook copy. Get in touch with us at :

business@bpbonline.com for more details.

At **www.bpbonline.com**, you can also read a collection of free technical articles, sign up for a range of free newsletters, and receive exclusive discounts and offers on BPB books and eBooks.

Piracy

If you come across any illegal copies of our works in any form on the internet, we would be grateful if you would provide us with the location address or website name. Please contact us at **business@bpbonline.com** with a link to the material.

If you are interested in becoming an author

If there is a topic that you have expertise in, and you are interested in either writing or contributing to a book, please visit **www.bpbonline.com**. We have worked with thousands of developers and tech professionals, just like you, to help them share their insights with the global tech community. You can make a general application, apply for a specific hot topic that we are recruiting an author for, or submit your own idea.

Reviews

Please leave a review. Once you have read and used this book, why not leave a review on the site that you purchased it from? Potential readers can then see and use your unbiased opinion to make purchase decisions. We at BPB can understand what you think about our products, and our authors can see your feedback on their book. Thank you!

For more information about BPB, please visit **www.bpbonline. com**.

Table of Contents

CHAPTER 1
Introduction to the Modern SAP Enterprise

Introduction

SAP customers often leverage code customizations as part of their enterprise transformation journey to tailor SAP solutions to fulfill their business needs. These customizations involve modifying, extending, or creating the business functionality of SAP applications by developing custom code. This is essential to aligning SAP software with unique business processes, industry requirements, or specific organization needs based on a customer's geography or global footprint. Development is not just about writing code.

A modern approach to the SAP enterprise involves keeping the core clean and building loosely coupled API-based applications that integrate with the customer's core **enterprise resource planning (ERP)** systems. There is often more than one system to integrate with. This approach reduces the operational burden of maintaining many ERP systems, efficiently upgrading and patching systems, optimizing performance, and pinpointing trouble before it begins in the enterprise.

SAP is the leading provider of ERP software since being founded in 1972. Over the course of five decades, SAP has evolved from providing systems and frameworks of packaged applications to industry-leading software and solutions, offered as a managed service, with a suite of products that enable customers to integrate with their internal has been the leading provider of ERP software since it was and develop new applications leveraging the latest cloud services the market has to offer.

We wrote this book to provide the reader with an overview of SAP's shift in delivering its flagship ERP software, the sizing and license requirements that customers should consider, the journey to either upgrading or initiating their ERP business transformation, leveraging native cloud services provided by cloud providers, and harnessing the power of GenAI in their ERP applications.

Structure

The topics covered in the chapter are as follows:

- Introducing SAP clean core methodology
- Evolution of the SAP development platform
- Introduction to SAP Cloud Platform extension tools

Objectives

By the end of this chapter, you will gain a comprehensive understanding of SAP's latest solutions and methodologies as of this book's writing. For those beginning their SAP journey, this chapter serves as an essential foundation, introducing key concepts and current best practices. You will learn critical SAP terminology, explore the platform's core solutions, understand SAP's emerging generative AI strategy, and discover the essential tools that will help you succeed in your SAP projects.

Introducing SAP clean core methodology

Many organizations have been using SAP for decades, and their systems have evolved over time. Here's an overview of the typical state of SAP systems in many enterprises.

SAP custom code and configuration

For decades, customers have been customizing the ERP core to accommodate their implementation to their business needs and business processes. Writing custom code to enhance and modify the standard functionality has been the usual course of action for almost all enterprises. The primary development language for SAP systems is SAP's **Advanced Business Application Programming (ABAP)**. Maintaining custom code not only involves boundary systems and resources, but it also requires dependency validations and configurations during major and minor releases, the utilization of SAP transport management, and a thorough understanding of SAP's business process design and development. It also involves ongoing activities to ensure that custom code remains functional, efficient, and compatible with system upgrades and changes.

Challenges with managing custom code

Managing custom code in SAP is a crucial aspect of ensuring system stability, security, and ease of maintenance. Effective management practices help SAP customers keep track of their custom developments, adapt to changing business requirements, and seamlessly integrate with future SAP updates. Here are common strategies SAP customers employ to manage their custom code:

- **System upgrades and S/4HANA conversion**: Managing custom code during system upgrades requires careful attention, particularly when transitioning to S/4HANA. Each new SAP software release necessitates a comprehensive impact analysis of existing custom code. This analysis identifies required modifications to maintain system compatibility, from adjusting code logic to adapting new data structures and replacing deprecated functionalities. The SAP ECC to S/4HANA transformation presents particular challenges. Organizations typically undertake extensive custom code analysis projects spanning multiple months to ensure successful adoption. While SAP provides tools like **Custom Code Migration and Analysis (CDMC)** to support this process, the scope of work remains substantial. Many organizations leverage specialized tools and frameworks developed by SAP partners to streamline their transformation journey.

- **SAP patching and support pack update**: SAP patching and support package updates are important for customers to remediate security vulnerabilities, known bugs, and performance issues. Custom code adds an extra burden of unit testing and integration testing of business scenarios during and after the support package is applied to SAP systems. It is important to test custom code after applying these updates to ensure a successful business outcome.

- **Ever-growing custom code**: Over the period of time, custom code becomes stale and unused in the system. There are many customers who do not retire their custom code even if the business process does not use it anymore. This is one of the biggest factors for maintaining the custom code in the long run. There is no governance around the custom code retirement and verification process. Old custom code can lead to hindrance in performance and increase operational issues.

- **Testing and quality assurance**: As part of maintenance activities, thoroughly test custom code changes to ensure they function correctly and do not introduce any new issues. This includes regression testing, integration testing, and performance testing. Maintaining a comprehensive test suite helps validate the stability and reliability of the custom code.

- **Performance monitoring and optimization**: Leveraging SAP tools to continuously monitor code performance, capturing and analyzing code execution in order to identify performance remediation, and data access pattern performance.

- **Version control systems:** SAP customers often use **version control systems** (**VCS**), such as Git or SAP's own Transport Organizer, to manage changes to custom code. This enables tracking of code versions, collaborative development, and the ability to roll back changes if needed.

- **Transport management system (TMS):** TMS is a key tool in SAP for managing the transport of custom code between different system landscapes, such as development, testing, and production environments. TMS ensures that changes are properly transported and synchronized across systems.

- **Code documentation:** Comprehensive documentation is vital for maintaining and evolving custom code over time. SAP customers implement a multi-layered documentation strategy, combining code comments, inline documentation, and dedicated documentation tools. This approach ensures that developers can quickly understand each custom object's purpose, implementation details, usage patterns, and system dependencies, facilitating efficient maintenance and knowledge transfer.

- **Change Request Management: Change Request Management (ChaRM)** is a part of SAP Solution Manager that helps manage the entire change control process, including custom developments. It provides features for request creation, approval workflows, and tracking changes throughout the development lifecycle.

- **Code reviews:** Performing regular code reviews helps ensure code quality, adherence to coding standards, and consistency. Code reviews are often conducted by development teams to identify issues early in the development process and share knowledge among team members.

- **Code quality tools:** SAP customers use code quality tools, such as SAP Code Inspector or third-party tools, to analyze custom code for performance, security, and adherence to best practices. These tools help identify areas for improvement and ensure that code meets established standards.

- **Test management:** Robust testing practices are crucial for custom code management. SAP customers use testing tools and frameworks to perform unit testing, integration testing, and regression testing to ensure custom developments work as intended and do not negatively impact existing functionality.

- **Retrofitting:** Retrofitting is a process where changes made in a higher SAP system landscape (e.g., production) are selectively applied to lower landscapes (e.g., development or testing). This ensures consistency across environments and reduces the risk of errors during transports.

- **Code archiving:** Over time, custom code can accumulate, leading to increased system complexity. SAP customers may implement code archiving strategies to identify and archive unused or obsolete code, reducing system overhead and improving performance.

- **Custom code lifecycle management:** Managing the custom code lifecycle involves tracking changes from development to production, including proper approvals and documentation. It ensures that changes are made in a controlled and traceable manner, aligning with organizational policies and compliance requirements.

- **Regular audits:** Conducting regular audits of custom code helps identify security vulnerabilities, performance bottlenecks, and adherence to coding standards. Audits contribute to the ongoing improvement and optimization of custom developments.

- **Knowledge transfer and training:** Knowledge transfer sessions and ongoing training for development teams are essential for maintaining a skilled workforce that can effectively manage and enhance custom code. This helps ensure that the development team is aware of best practices and the latest SAP technologies.

Embark on your clean core journey

SAP generally recommends that customers minimize all customizations to their standard software solutions in order to take full advantage of SAP's best practices, benefit from future upgrades seamlessly, and avoid potential challenges associated with extensive customizations. Customers have always embarked on large-scale business transformation projects where their partners have introduced templates and accelerators to prepare SAP for their business processes. Customers have been customizing the SAP core systems for decades; hence, moving to a clean core is a **journey** that requires careful analysis of existing business processes and the purpose-built adoption of new cloud-native services. This eliminates the reliance on custom code and adopts standards-based services like SAP **Business Technology Platform** (**BTP**) or Partner Solutions. Taking the path of keeping the core clean and developing around the core SAP ERP with extensibility requires customer-specific analysis of their business needs and utilizing SAP tools and services to solve the business needs. There are various advantages of adopting to clean core methodology:

- **Increase operational efficiency in areas of system upgrades, system maintenance, and Regression testing**: If custom code directly modifies or enhances standard SAP objects (for example, modifying standard programs or database tables), these modifications may become incompatible with the upgraded system. The upgraded objects may have different structures or logic, causing issues with the custom code. These lead to unplanned downtimes and business impacts.

- **Cost of managing custom code**: There is always a need to maintain custom code separately in terms of project releases to make sure business functionalities are not impacted. This is not a frugal use of time for experienced developers trying to fix production support issues caused by custom code conflicts across the projects in the organization.

- **Impact on innovation and technology adoption**: Custom code written over the period of years by many different developers in organizations is hard to analyze and replace. Changing or replacing these custom codes to adopt the latest innovation and technology, along with business continuity, is one of the toughest asks in the industry.

- **Performance Issues leading to business impacts**: Custom codes written over decades are tough to analyze for performance challenges. Many times, developers write their code snippets to build an application over time, leading to performance issues in the system.

Another concept that will help you understand more about the clean core is the idea of low-code and no-code development.

Introducing low-code and no-code development

SAP offers **low-code and no-code (LCNC)** development capabilities to enable business users and developers to build applications quickly and easily without extensive coding knowledge. These tools aim to accelerate application development, improve productivity, and empower business users to create their own solutions. LCNC environments offer a simplified building experience, but behind the scenes, they use the same kind of code and tooling as traditional development environments and are, therefore, capable of delivering equivalent results. Applications built with LCNC have no inherent compromises or disadvantages compared to apps built with traditional development environments.

LCNC refers to a new style of visual programming that makes it possible to develop applications without the use of coding languages, which greatly reduces the barrier of entry for anyone looking to take up application development. To differentiate between the two aspects:

- **Low-code** uses both a traditional programming language-based environment combined with no-code platforms and is used by developers with at least basic technical knowledge.

- **No-code** is simpler, and it fully replaces the traditional programming language-based tooling with a suite of visual development tools (for example, drag-and-drop components) and can be used by technical and non-technical people alike, such as citizen developers.

As per a recent IDC survey, there will be a 15% shortage of full-time developers worldwide compared with demand. LCNC development improves staff retention by 44% and simplifies developer experience by 36%, overall leading to better innovation and digitization of enterprise business processes and enhanced return on investment.

Advantages of low code-no code

SAP ABAP and traditional app developers will benefit from learning the best practices and principles of leveraging LCNC services to develop their business applications. Here are the key advantages:

- **Time to value:** The traditional way of development has always been longer, with value realization being slow. The LCNC technique accelerates time to value in building business applications by using industry best practices and **Line of Business (LoB)** specific pre-built content. Standardization of framework and content helps to increase agility and speed to deliver business applications.

- **Reduce total cost**: This technique helps reduce the total cost of developing and supporting enterprise software to support business processes across the organization. Since the pre-built templates and business content are used, this reduces the resources and time needed to develop the software, and standardization of content helps reduce the operational cost.

- **Enhanced return on investment**: The LCNC technique also helps with better ROI for the investment as time to market and value is quicker, and it takes less effort and cost to build and digitize the enterprise applications.

Increased innovation and adoption: The LCNC technique makes it easier for an enterprise to adopt digital transformation and a path to optimized business processes with reduced technical debt from old and legacy applications. This helps customers adopt the path of continuous innovation for faster business outcomes.

Evolution of the SAP development platform

SAP provides several development tools and technologies that facilitate the customization, extension, and development of applications within the S/4HANA environment. Here are some key development tools used in SAP S/4HANA:

- **ABAP Development Tools (ADT):** ADT is an **Integrated Development Environment (IDE)** for SAP's proprietary programming language, ABAP. ADT provides a rich set of features for developing, testing, and debugging ABAP code. It includes editors, object browsers, code completion, and performance analysis tools. In the past, SAP had its SAPGUI-based development environment, the ABAP Workbench, while also providing integrated access to all ABAP development objects. It is particularly valued by developers for features such as versioning and the where-used list, which shows exactly where a particular object has been reused by other objects.

  SAP launched the ADT for Eclipse in recognition of the fact that an SAP development project will need beyond pure ABAP into the HANA or SAP UI5 space. Eclipse provides this common ground, and ABAP developers have the choice between working with the ADT for Eclipse (ADT) and the classic SAPGUI-based ABAP Workbench.

- **SAP Fiori:** SAP Fiori is a framework that simplifies the development of user interfaces for SAP S/4HANA applications. It offers pre-built UI templates and controls that generate Fiori-like user interfaces based on metadata configurations. Fiori Elements significantly reduces the amount of UI development effort required by providing consistent and responsive UIs for common application scenarios.

Here are some key aspects of the SAP Fiori framework:

- **Pre-built templates**: Fiori Elements provides a collection of pre-built templates for common application scenarios, such as list reports, object pages, and overview pages. These templates come with predefined layouts, navigation patterns, and UI patterns, reducing the need for manual UI development.

- **Data-driven UI generation**: Fiori Elements leverages metadata annotations, such as those defined in the OData service, to automatically generate the UI based on the underlying data model. This allows for consistent and efficient UI generation without the need for extensive manual coding.

- **Smart controls and annotations**: Fiori Elements incorporates smart controls that can automatically handle common UI patterns, such as filtering, sorting, and grouping. These controls use annotations in the OData service to determine their behavior and provide a more intelligent and interactive user experience.

- **Responsive design**: Fiori Elements are designed to be responsive, adapting the UI layout and controls to different screen sizes and devices. This ensures a consistent and optimized user experience across desktops, tablets, and mobile devices.

- **Integration with SAPUI5 and SAP Fiori**: Fiori Elements are built on top of SAPUI5, a JavaScript framework for building web applications. It leverages SAP Fiori design principles and guidelines, ensuring that the UIs created with Fiori Elements align with the Fiori user experience.

- **Extensibility and customization**: Fiori Elements also allow for customization and extension of the generated UIs. Developers can modify the UI by adding annotations, extending the UI annotations, or even implementing custom logic to meet specific business requirements.

Introduction to SAP Cloud Platform extension tools

SAP Cloud Platform offers a range of tools and services for extending and customizing SAP S/4HANA applications. These include SAP Web IDE, which provides a browser-based development environment for building Fiori apps and extensions, as well as services like SAP Cloud Platform Integration and SAP Cloud Platform Workflow for integrating and extending S/4HANA functionality. We would like you to familiarize yourself with a few basic SAP Cloud Platform extension tools. They are as follows:

- **In-App extensions with classic development tools:** SAP In-App Extensions refer to the capability provided by SAP to extend the functionality of their applications directly within the existing user interface or context of the application. It allows customers and partners to enhance and customize SAP applications without modifying the core codebase.

  Here are some key aspects of SAP In-App extensions:

  o **Contextual extension:** In-App Extensions enable the addition of custom fields, logic, and UI elements within the context of an existing SAP application. These extensions are tightly integrated with the standard application and can leverage the existing data model, business logic, and user interface.

  o **Key user tools:** SAP provides tools and frameworks that empower key users (non-developers) to create and manage In-App Extensions. These tools often include a user-friendly UI for defining custom fields, modifying screens, configuring business rules, and creating custom reports.

  o **No core modification:** In-App Extensions are designed to be non-invasive and do not require modifications to the core codebase of the SAP application. This ensures that the extensions can be seamlessly upgraded and maintained across system updates and new releases.

  o **Supported by SAP APIs:** In-App Extensions utilize SAP APIs (Application Programming Interfaces) and extension points provided by SAP applications. These APIs expose specific integration points and hooks that enable custom functionality to be added in a controlled and supported manner.

  o **Enhancing existing processes:** In-App Extensions allow for the extension of existing SAP processes and functionalities to meet specific business requirements. This could involve adding custom validation rules, creating new screens for data entry, integrating with external systems, or generating custom reports.

  o **Lifecycle management:** SAP provides tools and mechanisms to manage the lifecycle of In-App extensions.

This includes versioning, transport management, and deployment mechanisms to ensure that extensions can be developed, tested, and moved across different system landscapes.

- **Side-by-Side extensibility**: SAP Side-by-Side Extensibility is an approach that allows customers to extend and enhance SAP applications by developing and deploying custom functionalities outside of the core system landscape. It enables organizations to innovate and meet specific business requirements without making modifications to the standard SAP software.

Here are some key aspects of SAP Side-by-Side extensibility:

  o **Decoupled customization**: With Side-by-Side extensibility, custom functionalities are developed and deployed separately from the core SAP system. This decoupling ensures that customizations can be maintained and upgraded independently, without impacting the stability and supportability of the core system.

  o **Integration with SAP applications**: Side-by-Side extensibility leverages integration technologies and APIs provided by SAP to establish communication and data exchange between the custom extensions and the SAP applications. This allows for seamless integration and collaboration between custom functionalities and the core SAP system.

  o **Cloud and on-premises deployment**: Side-by-Side extensibility supports deployment options both in the cloud and on-premises. Custom functionalities can be developed using cloud-based services, such as SAP Cloud Platform, or using on-premises development tools and platforms, depending on the organization's infrastructure and requirements.

  o **Extensibility frameworks**: SAP provides extensibility frameworks and tools that facilitate Side-by-Side Extensibility. These frameworks, such as SAP Cloud Platform Extension Suite and SAP **Cloud Application Programming Model (CAP),** offer development guidelines, runtime environments, and services for building and deploying custom extensions.

o **Custom business processes**: Side-by-Side extensibility allows organizations to implement custom business processes and functionalities that are specific to their unique requirements. This includes building custom UIs, integrating with external systems, implementing custom workflows, and creating additional reporting and analytics capabilities.

o **Security and governance**: SAP provides security mechanisms and governance frameworks to ensure that Side-by-Side extensions adhere to organizational policies and meet security standards. This includes authentication, authorization, and data protection measures to safeguard the integrity and confidentiality of the extended systems.

SAP Business Technology Platform

SAP BTP is a foundational technology service offered by SAP for the Intelligent, sustainable Enterprise, covering aspects of the following:

* **Application development**: Developers can utilize SAP BTP to build and extend applications, keep the core clean, and utilize the Low code and No code development mechanism we read about earlier.

* **Integration**: Developers have utilized SAP PI/PO for their integration/API development needs in the past. SAP offers the Integration Suite and APIM to integrate and accelerate business outcomes.

* **Automation**: Automation is the key aspect of every enterprise to optimize its business process and bring more efficiency. BTP provides a set of services like workflow management, **Robotic Process Automation** (RPA) (Part of SAP Build), Process monitoring and analytics, etc., to help customers achieve optimization and efficiency in their business processes across the enterprise.

* **Data and analytics**: SAP BTP offers data management services like Datasphere, Analytics, and planning, and even database management, allowing businesses to store, manage, and analyze their data efficiently.

- **IoT, AI/ML and Generative AI**: IoT, AI, and ML services offered by SAP BTP includes SAP AI Core, prebuilt AI Models, IoT and Big data applications.

We will talk about the impact of Generative AI in the upcoming chapters. How Generative AI is becoming a revolution in providing intelligent business outcomes, along with helping the developer community in speeding up the common development aspects of enterprise projects.

SAP BTP offers a range of development tools and services that can be leveraged for SAP S/4HANA development. This includes the SAP CAP, which provides a set of tools and guidelines for building enterprise-grade applications with consistent data models, service APIs, and user interfaces. Before we dive deeper into the development capabilities of the BTP platform. Let us now focus on two different programming models provided by SAP for developing applications on their platform:

SAP Cloud Application Programming Model

SAP CAP is a framework that enables developers to build multi-tiered cloud applications that run on SAP Cloud Platform. CAP supports various programming languages, including JavaScript and TypeScript. It provides a model-driven development approach, allowing developers to define their data models, services, and UIs using **Domain-specific languages** like **Core Data Services (CDS)**. It supports a range of databases, such as SAP HANA, SQLite, PostgreSQL, and others.

SAP S/4HANA ABAP RESTful Application Programming Model

SAP S/4HANA ABAP **RESTful Application Programming** (RAP) Model is a framework specifically designed for building applications on the SAP S/4HANA platform using the ABAP programming language. It follows a data-centric development approach, where the data models are defined using ABAP Dictionary structures and annotations. RAP applications are built as **ABAP Managed Database Procedures (AMDP)** and leverage the power of the SAP HANA database. It provides a set of predefined services for handling **Create, Read, Update, and Delete (CRUD)** operations on the data models.

RAP supports the development of OData-based services that expose the application's functionality to external systems. It offers features like automatic data access, authorization checks, and service exposure based on annotations.

Generative AI

Generative AI is the next-generation Artificial Intelligence platform where it is not only provides AI/ML-based business insights but also generates new, creative, realistic content that can be used in enterprise business processes to make it more intelligent, dynamic, and agile. It is very important for customers and readers to understand that the first level of automation/efficiency in the business process can be brought in by utilizing tools and services like (RPA, part of SAP built-in BTP), workflow management, and DevOps tools and services offered SAP and cloud provider like Amazon Web Services.

Next came the artificial intelligence and machine learning services, which help build systems/machines that can perform intelligent tasks for the Enterprise, including learning, recognizing patterns, problem-solving, and making decisions. Machine learning is part of the AI ecosystem for training the AI model. In ML models, you feed the algorithm with data and let it learn the patterns and make predictions and decisions based on the data. It helps customers improve business process efficiency and performance.

Generative AI is designed to generate content, summaries, images, and videos based on the learning models they were trained on. Cloud providers like Amazon Web Services are making big investments in their Generative AI offerings like Amazon Bedrock, Code Whisperer. Microsoft has invested in OpenAI to boost its Generative AI offerings, and Google has launched Google AI.

Generative AI ramps up the art of possibility in every industry and for customers, helping in areas like Intelligent chatbots, summarization (text extraction), text generation to increase productivity, image generation and video generation and more.

From a development perspective, the most intuitive part of GenAI is automatic code generation in real-time based on your business scenario description. SAP is offering GenAI through SAP AI Core for customers to utilize GenAI capability through the BTP. We mentioned Amazon Code Whisperer, which is trained on billions of lines of code and can generate code suggestions in real-time.

At the time of publishing this book, SAP released the *Business AI* suite of tools for customers who have chosen to embark on their journey to RISE or GROW with SAP. We will discuss these upgrades later in this book. SAP Joule is an interactive generative AI copilot designed to assist customers with their interactions with the many SAP systems and can generate code for customers who are going to be using SAP systems in the cloud. Joule will be embedded throughout SAP's cloud enterprise portfolio, delivering proactive and contextualized insights from across the breadth and depth of SAP solutions and third-party sources. By quickly sorting through and contextualizing data from multiple systems to surface smarter insights, Joule helps people get work done faster and drive better business outcomes in a secure, compliant way. Joule delivers on SAP's proven track record of revolutionary technology that drives real results. SAP Joule and the many agents that will interact with Joule are all part of SAP's Business AI toolkit that we will cover in later chapters.

Conclusion

In this chapter, we have taken a comprehensive journey through the modern SAP enterprise landscape. We started by exploring the historical context of SAP development, highlighting the challenges of managing custom code in SAP systems. We then introduced the concept of the SAP clean core methodology, which aims to minimize customizations and leverage standardized, cloud-based solutions.

We delved into the evolution of SAP's development platform, discussing key tools like ADT and SAP Fiori. We also explored the SAP Cloud Platform extension tools, including In-App extensions and Side-by-Side extensibility, which provide flexible options for customizing and extending SAP applications.

The chapter also introduced the SAP BTP, a foundational service that covers various aspects of enterprise technology, including application development, integration, automation, data and analytics, and AI/ ML capabilities. We discussed two important programming models: the SAP CAP and the SAP S/4HANA ABAP **RESTful Application Programming** Model (**RAP**).

Finally, we touched upon the emerging field of Generative AI and its potential impact on SAP development and business processes. We highlighted SAP's initiatives in this area, including the introduction of Joule, a new AI assistant designed to enhance productivity across SAP's cloud portfolio.

This chapter has laid the groundwork for understanding SAP enterprise solutions' current state and future direction. In the next chapter, we will study the details of RISE and GROW, SAP's strategic initiatives for cloud transformation. We will explore how these programs can help enterprises transition to the cloud and leverage SAP's latest technologies. We'll also discuss the decision-making process for selecting the right SAP solution for your enterprise, considering factors such as business needs, existing infrastructure, and long-term strategic goals.

Multiple choice questions

1. **What is the primary goal of SAP's clean core methodology?**

   a. To maximize custom code development

   b. To minimize customizations and maintain standard solutions

   c. To increase technical debt

   d. To encourage direct core modifications

2. **Which challenges do organizations face when managing custom code in SAP systems?**

   a. System upgrades and compatibility issues

   b. Performance monitoring and optimization

   c. Testing and quality assurance

   d. All of the above

3. **What is a key advantage of adopting low-code/no-code development?**

   a. Increased development complexity

   b. Reduced time to value

   c. Higher maintenance costs

   d. Limited integration capabilities

4. **In the context of SAP development, what does CAP stand for?**

   a. Core Application Platform

   b. Cloud Application Programming

c. Custom ABAP Programming

d. Central Administration Portal

5. **What is the primary purpose of the SAP Integration Suite?**

a. Database management

b. User interface development

c. Application and process integration

d. Code compilation

6. **Which component is NOT part of SAP's AI portfolio?**

a. SAP AI Core

b. SAP AI Launchpad

c. SAP AI Engine

d. Generative AI Hub

7. **What is a key characteristic of RAP (RESTful Application Programming Model)?**

a. It only supports cloud deployments

b. It's specifically designed for ABAP development

c. It doesn't support OData services

d. It requires Java programming

8. **Which statement best describes SAP's Generative AI strategy?**

a. It focuses solely on code generation

b. It integrates with existing SAP applications through Joule

c. It only works with on-premises systems

d. It's limited to text processing

9. **What is the primary function of SAP Business Technology Platform (BTP)?**

a. Hardware provisioning

b. Network management

c. Application development and integration

d. Database administration only

10. **Which of the following is a key benefit of maintaining a clean core?**

    a. Increased operational efficiency

    b. Easier system upgrades

    c. Reduced regression testing efforts

    d. All of the above

Answers

1. b

   Explanation: The clean core methodology aims to minimize customizations to standard SAP solutions, enabling customers to take full advantage of SAP's best practices, benefit from future upgrades seamlessly, and avoid potential challenges associated with extensive customizations.

2. d

   Explanation: Organizations face multiple challenges when managing custom code, including compatibility issues during upgrades, the need for continuous performance monitoring and optimization, and extensive testing and quality assurance requirements to ensure system stability.

3. b

   Explanation: Low-code/no-code development accelerates time to value by using industry best practices and pre-built content, enabling faster application development and deployment compared to traditional development approaches.

4. b

   Explanation: Cloud Application Programming (CAP) is SAP's framework for building enterprise-grade applications and services, providing a consistent end-to-end programming model.

5. c

   Explanation: SAP Integration Suite is designed to enable seamless integration between different applications and processes, providing tools and capabilities for connecting various systems and services.

6. c

   Explanation: SAP AI Engine is not a part of SAP's AI portfolio. The main components include SAP AI Core, SAP AI Launchpad, and Generative AI Hub.

7. b

   Explanation: RAP is specifically designed for developing applications in the ABAP environment, providing a framework for building SAP Fiori apps and Web APIs using ABAP programming.

8. b

   Explanation: SAP's Generative AI strategy focuses on integrating AI capabilities across its application suite through Joule, providing contextual assistance and enhancing user experiences.

9. c

   Explanation: SAP BTP serves as a comprehensive platform for application development, integration, and extension of SAP applications, providing tools and services for building and connecting enterprise solutions.

10. d

    Explanation: Maintaining a clean core provides multiple benefits, including increased operational efficiency, easier system upgrades, and reduced regression testing efforts, as it minimizes custom code and keeps the system closer to standard.

Join our book's Discord space

Join the book's Discord Workspace for Latest updates, Offers, Tech happenings around the world, New Release and Sessions with the Authors:

https://discord.bpbonline.com

CHAPTER 2

Overview of SAP's Latest Offers, RISE and GROW

Introduction

The enterprise software landscape has undergone a remarkable transformation, and SAP has been at the forefront of this evolution. From its origins in traditional perpetual licensing to today's dynamic subscription-based models through RISE and GROW with SAP, this journey reflects not just a change in deployment methods but a fundamental shift in how organizations approach their digital transformation.

In this chapter, we will explore this compelling evolution of SAP deployment models and examine how it has revolutionized the development lifecycle, tools, and services that support modern enterprises. You will discover how the transition from on-premises solutions to cloud-based services has opened new possibilities for innovation and agility. We will delve into the comprehensive ecosystem of the SAP Business Technology Platform, exploring how it enables organizations to extend, integrate, and optimize their business processes.

From the democratization of development through low-code/no-code solutions to the integration of cutting-edge technologies like artificial intelligence and sustainability tools, we will uncover how these changes are shaping the future of enterprise software. Join us on this journey through SAP's transformation and learn how these advances are enabling organizations to become more resilient, innovative, and ready for tomorrow's challenges.

Structure

The chapter covers the following topics:

- Evolution of SAP deployment framework
- Customers Cloud ERP journey
- Introduction to RISE with SAP
- Introduction to GROW with SAP
- Additional components

Objectives

After completing this chapter, you will embark on a comprehensive journey through SAP's evolution in the cloud era. You will gain the ability to trace SAP's transformation from its traditional on-premises roots to its modern cloud-first approach, understanding the pivotal moments that shaped this evolution.

You will develop a clear understanding of SAP's flagship offerings, RISE with SAP and GROW with SAP, and be able to guide organizations in choosing the right path for their digital transformation. This includes mastering the distinctions between public and private cloud editions and knowing when each is most appropriate for different business scenarios.

Your journey will take you through SAP's modern extensibility framework, where you will learn to leverage both side-by-side and In-App extensions using the SAP Business Technology Platform. You will understand how to harness the power of low-code/no-code solutions through SAP Build, enabling rapid innovation while maintaining a clean core.

The chapter will equip you with knowledge of SAP's comprehensive cloud components, from mobile solutions to advanced financial management tools. You will understand how artificial intelligence, through SAP Joule, and sustainability solutions are reshaping business operations.

Finally, you will grasp how the **Cloud Platform Enterprise Agreement** (**CPEA**) provides the flexibility organizations need to explore and implement various SAP Business Technology Platform services, ensuring they can adapt their technology stack as their needs evolve.

Evolution of SAP deployment framework

In the last section, we discussed various shifts in development strategies, such as the clean core approach, the rise of Low-Code and No-Code Development, and the integration of cloud-based tools, services, and applications. Examples include the SAP Business Technology Platform (covered in detail in *Chapter 3, SAP Business Technology Platform and Cloud Provider Integration*) and tools and services designed for cloud-native environments provided by Cloud Service Providers like AWS. These have been adopted to address business challenges across various industries and sectors.

The evolution of SAP's deployment approaches has seen significant changes in response to advancements in technology and shifting business requirements. SAP, an acronym for systems, applications, and products in data processing, is recognized worldwide for its leadership in **enterprise resource planning** (**ERP**) software. The following is a concise summary of how SAP's deployment models have transformed over time:

- **On-premises deployment (From 1972):** In the beginning, SAP provided its software solely for on-premises use. Customers would install and operate the software on their own hardware, overseen by their in-house IT personnel. SAP R/1, the initial version, was introduced in 1972. SAP then released R/2 in 1979, broadening its reach beyond Germany.

- **Shift to client-server model (From 1992):** In 1992, SAP moved to a client-server model with the introduction of SAP R/3. This framework facilitated the distribution of applications across different computing tiers, generally including a database server, an application server, and a client user interface. This advancement yielded greater flexibility and improved access over traditional mainframe configurations.

- **Web-enabled features (Early 2000s):** During the early 2000s, SAP started to incorporate web functionality into its offerings, culminating in the creation of *mySAP.com*. This integration permitted users to operate SAP applications via a web browser, thereby enhancing convenience and providing greater flexibility.

- **Move towards cloud computing (2010s):** With the rise of cloud computing, SAP started offering cloud-based solutions. This started with Business ByDesign in 2007 and was followed by the acquisition of SuccessFactors in 2011, a cloud-based human capital management solution.

- **Introduction of SAP HANA and S/4HANA (Since 2011):** The debut of SAP HANA in 2011 marked a pivotal advancement with its high-speed in-memory database technology. Following this, SAP S/4HANA was unveiled in 2015 as the next-gen business suite, optimized to run solely on SAP HANA, providing options for both on-premises and cloud deployments.

- **Further Cloud expansion and hybrid models (Late 2010s onwards)**: SAP continued to expand its cloud offerings with acquisitions like Concur and Fieldglass, and by enhancing its own cloud capabilities. Many businesses started adopting a hybrid model, using a mix of on-premises and cloud solutions to meet their specific needs.

- **Rise of intelligent technologies and integration (2020s):** SAP has been integrating artificial intelligence, machine learning, and **Internet of Things (IoT)** capabilities into its solutions, offering more advanced and intelligent ERP systems. The focus is increasingly on the seamless integration of various business processes and data analytics to drive decision-making.

Throughout its evolution, SAP has remained at the forefront of technological innovation, adapting its offerings to align with emerging trends and shifts in the marketplace. Initially focused on standard on-premises deployments, SAP has expanded its portfolio to include a range of flexible solutions that leverage cloud computing and offer hybrid capabilities, blending on-premises and cloud functionalities. Now, SAP is advancing into the realm of intelligent technologies, integrating AI, machine learning, and advanced analytics into its suite of products. This strategic direction not only reflects SAP's commitment to innovation but also exemplifies broader trends in the

IT industry, where enterprise software is increasingly becoming more intelligent, connected, and user-centric, offering businesses enhanced insights, automation, and efficiency.

Another facet of the current technology trend is the growing eagerness among customers to embrace cloud services, contemporary integration, and development frameworks. Additionally, there is a trend towards adopting a modular approach for addressing business challenges and shaping the IT landscape. This approach allows for greater flexibility and scalability, enabling businesses to adapt rapidly to changing market conditions and technological advancements. It reflects a shift in strategy towards more agile, resilient, and customizable solutions in enterprise technology.

Amidst a wave of technological progress and a customer-centric shift towards refining the IT landscape for cost savings, retiring legacy systems, and transforming business processes for enhanced operational efficiency, in January 2021, SAP introduced RISE with SAP. This initiative is designed to support customers in prioritizing their business needs. RISE with SAP offers a holistic business transformation as a service, encapsulating the technical migration to a simplified, cost-effective cloud environment and facilitating the modernization of business processes. This solution aligns with the strategic move to streamline operations, reduce complexity, and position businesses to better leverage new technologies to drive effective business outcomes.

Customers Cloud ERP journey

Businesses across different industries, while having their unique operational demands, also share some core expectations. A primary concern for all is the implementation of strong security protocols. Compliance with local and governmental regulatory standards is another universal requirement. Furthermore, these organizations often grapple with the complexities of managing integrated systems across various functions. To successfully navigate these challenges, they need access to tools that allow for the customization of solutions to align with their specific business objectives and requirements.

Businesses looking for standardized processes that are routinely upgraded to the newest version and those who favor their cloud provider managing the infrastructure will find SAP S/4HANA Cloud, public edition, highly suitable. This cloud-native ERP solution brings the latest industry practices and continuous innovation to the table.

It provides a smooth and updated experience for companies focusing on efficiency and simplicity in their cloud strategies, ensuring they stay ahead with the most recent technological developments and best practices relevant to their industry.

For customers who require extensive customization in their workflows, prefer to progress with innovation at a pace that suits them, and desire more autonomy over their systems, the SAP S/4HANA Cloud, private edition, is an excellent choice. Tailored to accommodate the unique transformational path of each organization, this cloud ERP solution provides a highly flexible and customizable platform. It caters specifically to the individual needs and innovation timelines of businesses, ensuring their unique requirements are met with precision and control.

The differentiated approaches are illustrated in the following figure:

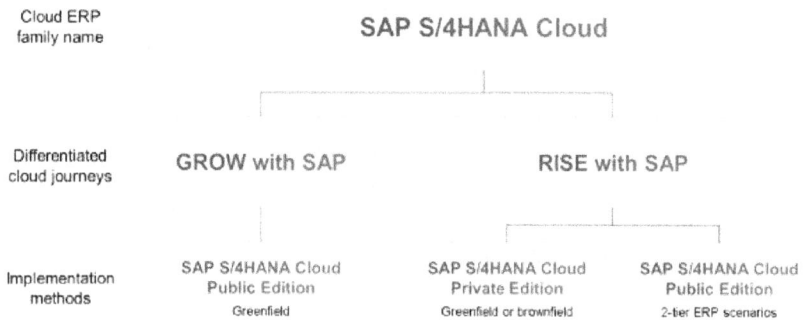

Cloud ERP family name	**SAP S/4HANA Cloud**		
Differentiated cloud journeys	**GROW with SAP**	**RISE with SAP**	
Implementation methods	SAP S/4HANA Cloud Public Edition Greenfield	SAP S/4HANA Cloud Private Edition Greenfield or brownfield	SAP S/4HANA Cloud Public Edition 2-tier ERP scenarios

Figure 2.1: RISE with SAP and GROW with SAP

Introduction to RISE with SAP

In January 2021, SAP unveiled RISE with SAP, a tailored initiative aimed at steering organizations through the intricacies of digital transformation. This offering serves as a full-package solution, delivering an intelligent and personalized roadmap for businesses to transition into nimble, cloud-based enterprises.

Expanding on this, RISE with SAP encompasses a suite of services and tools that address various aspects of a company's shift to digital:

- **Simplify Cloud journey**: RISE with SAP acts as a strategic partner for businesses looking to transfer their digital infrastructure to a robust and secure cloud platform. This service simplifies the migration process by providing comprehensive assistance, which includes detailed planning, execution, and post-migration support. Expert consultants from SAP offer tailored guidance that aligns with industry-specific best practices, ensuring a seamless transition with minimal disruption to daily operations. Additionally, RISE with SAP includes tools to automate parts of the migration, thorough security measures to safeguard data, and strategies to optimize cloud resource utilization post-transition. The aim is not only to move a business's digital assets to the cloud but also to enhance its performance and scalability, setting a foundation for future innovation and growth.

- **Enhancing technical and operational durability:** The transition to the cloud through RISE with SAP equips businesses with a fortified framework capable of withstanding variable market conditions and unforeseen disturbances. The cloud's inherent scalability allows for an agile response to shifts in demand, facilitating expansion or contraction of resources as needed. This resilience is further bolstered by the cloud's distributed architecture, which ensures business continuity by mitigating the impact of localized failures. RISE with SAP's cloud solutions is designed to support uninterrupted operations, even during high-traffic periods or in the event of technical challenges, ensuring that businesses maintain continuous service delivery. Additionally, cloud environments can offer improved data recovery and backup solutions, further contributing to operational robustness. In an era where adaptability and reliability are paramount, RISE with SAP provides businesses with the tools to build a resilient operational model that supports long-term stability and growth.

- **Streamlining the IT framework:** RISE with SAP is meticulously crafted to declutter the IT environment for businesses. It strategically aids in phasing out outdated legacy systems that frequently contribute to operational inefficiency. By doing so, it diminishes the intricate web of older technologies that can stifle quick adaptation and impede innovation. The service streamlines processes and integrates modern, cloud-based solutions that unify disparate systems and data silos, leading to a more cohesive and manageable IT architecture. This simplification process not only enhances system interoperability but also promotes a more agile IT operation, enabling faster response to new opportunities and challenges. Moreover, a less complex IT landscape can reduce maintenance costs and redirect resources toward innovation and growth, thus fostering an environment where businesses can thrive in the digital age with greater flexibility and a renewed focus on strategic initiatives.

- **Business process optimization**: RISE with SAP capitalizes on SAP's extensive expertise across various sectors to empower companies to refine their fundamental operations. This re-engineering effort is aimed at enhancing efficiency and effectiveness, tapping into the power of data analytics and intelligent process insights. With RISE with SAP, businesses can dissect and reconstruct their workflows, eliminate redundancies, and identify opportunities for automation. This optimization is underpinned by sophisticated analytics that provide deep visibility into operational performance, enabling data-driven decisions. The service encourages the adoption of best practices tailored to the unique processes and challenges of each industry, fostering a culture of continuous improvement. As a result, businesses can achieve streamlined operations, improved customer experiences, and a stronger competitive edge. In a broader sense, RISE with SAP does not just adjust processes; it transforms them to be more agile, transparent, and aligned with strategic business outcomes.

- **Financial strategy transformation**: RISE with SAP facilitates a significant shift in financial strategy for businesses by transitioning investments from **capital expenditure (CapEx)** to **operational expenditure (OpEx)**. This shift to a more predictable spending model allows for improved budgeting and forecasting, as costs become more regular and aligned with usage rather than requiring significant upfront investments in infrastructure and licensing. The OpEx model characteristic of cloud services offers scalability and flexibility, meaning businesses can adjust their costs in relation to their needs and growth. This not only aids in streamlining financial planning but also potentially liberates capital for reinvestment in other areas of the business that can drive innovation, enhance customer experiences, or enter new markets. By reducing the financial barriers associated with large-scale IT investments, RISE with SAP enables companies to be more dynamic and responsive to market opportunities and challenges.

By weaving together these strategic components, RISE with SAP does not merely transition businesses to cloud infrastructure; it thoroughly reinvents them as forward-thinking, intelligent enterprises ready to navigate the future. This initiative embodies SAP's dedication to facilitating client adaptation in an increasingly digital era, enabling businesses to attain unprecedented levels of operational efficiency, drive innovation, and enhance customer satisfaction.

Expanding on this, RISE with SAP is more than a cloud migration tool; it is a comprehensive transformation package that equips businesses with advanced analytics, process insights, and adaptable infrastructure. This allows for real-time decision-making, automation of routine tasks, and the agility to pivot according to market trends and customer needs. The emphasis on a modular and flexible IT environment means businesses can rapidly integrate new technologies and services as they emerge, staying ahead in a competitive landscape.

Furthermore, the shift from capital to OpEx reshapes the financial model of IT, making cutting-edge technology accessible without prohibitive upfront costs. This change unlocks potential for investments in areas critical to business growth and differentiation, such as research and development, marketing, and customer experience enhancements.

In essence, RISE with SAP is a testament to SAP's vision of helping clients build a resilient, adaptable, and innovative business that not only thrives today but is also poised for tomorrow's challenges and opportunities. It is an enabler for businesses to become entities that do not just respond to the digital revolution but lead it. The package offering for RISE is described as follows:

RISE WITH SAP

SAP S/4HANA Cloud Private Edition

Add-on packages with specialized capabilities (e.g. industries, office of the CFO)

Category	Item	Base	Premium	Premium Plus
Extension, Integration, Automation	SAP Build Apps		✓	✓
	SAP Build Work Zone	✓	✓	✓
	SAP Build Process Automation		✓	✓
	CPEA credits for SAP BTP		✓	✓
Advanced financial management	Group Reporting	✓	✓	✓
	Group Reporting Data Collection	✓	✓	✓
	Cash Management			✓
	Receivables Management			✓
Intelligent Spend Business Network (ISBN)	SAP Business Network Supplier Portal		✓	✓
Artificial Intelligence, Data, Analytics	Joule	✓	✓	✓
	AI Units		✓	✓
	SAP Analytics Cloud Planning		✓	✓
	SAP Datasphere		✓	✓
Sustainability	SAP Sustainability Footprint Management			✓
	SAP Sustainability Control Tower			✓
Licensing	Digital Access	✓	✓	✓

Figure 2.2: Package offering for RISE (2024)

Development framework around RISE with SAP

The synergistic development framework that merges RISE with SAP and Cloud Service Providers like AWS forges a formidable alliance that unites SAP's expertise in business process transformation with the robust cloud infrastructure and technology. This helps to expedite the journey of digital transformation, drawing upon the unique advantages of each SAP and Cloud Service provider offering.

RISE with SAP contributes deep-rooted business process acumen, tailored industry insights, and a clear, actionable pathway for transformation. On the other hand, Cloud Service Providers like AWS deliver a comprehensive suite of cloud services. This includes elastic computing resources, cutting-edge data storage options, and a vast repertoire of analytics capabilities. The convergence of these services under one developmental umbrella provides a fertile ground for businesses to foster innovation at an accelerated pace, dynamically scale resources in alignment with business demands, and deploy solutions that enhance operational efficiency and organizational agility.

The development framework around RISE with SAP and Cloud Service Providers is designed not only to facilitate a smooth transition to the cloud but also to empower businesses to become more innovative, resilient, and customer-centric in their operations. It is a comprehensive approach that aligns with the current and future needs of businesses seeking to thrive in the digital marketplace.

Overall, the development framework that integrates RISE with SAP and AWS Cloud is not just a pathway to cloud migration; it is a comprehensive strategy to empower businesses with the agility, innovation, and customer focus needed to excel in today's digital economy and beyond. It embodies a future-ready approach, ensuring that enterprises are well-equipped to adapt and thrive in an evolving business landscape.

Customers can leverage the SAP Business Technology Platform and cloud services around areas of application development, data and analytics, integration, IoT, AI/ML, and Generative AI to bolster their business transformation around RISE with SAP.

SAP has bundled BTP services like SAP Build Work Zone, SAP Build Process Automation, SAP Build Apps, and SAP Signavio to get started in their innovation journey. RISE with SAP customers have the advantage of utilizing SAP Build, a low-code tooling solution, to enhance their ERP systems. SAP Build allows for the easy customization and extension of ERP functionalities through a user-friendly interface. This tool is particularly beneficial for businesses as described in the following figure. For customers to streamline their operations with minimal technical expertise required.

Figure 2.3: *SAP's Business Technology Platform Build Components (2024)*

Introduction to GROW with SAP

SAP announced GROW with SAP to make the move towards a Cloud ERP solution. GROW with SAP is an S/4HANA Public Cloud and SaaS offering of solutions.

The GROW with SAP initiative is specially designed to assist companies in maximizing the benefits of cloud ERP. It aims to instill confidence in customers about swiftly deploying technology that supports their ongoing growth, both effectively and efficiently. GROW with SAP encompasses a comprehensive package that includes solutions tailored for midsize businesses, support based on industry best practices, services that speed up adoption, and community and learning resources. This offering focuses on delivering a cost-efficient and rapid implementation process, equipping businesses with the tools and capabilities they need to scale and adapt in the future. The components for SAP GROW (base and premium editions) are indicated as follows

		Base	Premium
Extension, Integration, Automation	SAP Build Apps		✓
	SAP Build Work Zone	✓	✓
	SAP Build Process Automation	✓	✓
	CPEA credits for SAP BTP	✓	✓
Advanced financial management	Group Reporting	✓	✓
	Advanced Financial Close		✓
	Cash Management		✓
	Receivables Management		✓
	Ariba Buying, base edition	✓	✓
Intelligent Spend Business Network (ISBN)	Central Invoice Management		✓
	Inbound Processing		✓
	SAP Sales Cloud V2		✓
	Concur Expense Professional		✓
Artificial Intelligence, Data, Analytics	Joule	✓	✓
	AI Units	✓	✓
	SAP Analytics Cloud Planning		✓
Licensing	Digital Access	✓	✓

GROW WITH SAP

SAP S/4HANA Cloud
Public Edition

+ Add-on packages with specialized capabilities
(e.g. industries, office of the CFO)

Figure 2.4: GROW with SAP application modules (2024)

As stated by SAP, the GROW with SAP packages have been designed to support the priorities of customers who want to adopt cloud ERP with speed, predictability, and continuous innovation. Customers can choose between the Base and Premium editions with optional add-on packages for specialized capabilities.

The Base edition is best for smaller and midsize organizations or emerging economies at a lower price point. It includes complimentary licenses to SAP BTP, some finance entitlements, and access to Ariba Buying, base edition to support sourcing and procurement activities.

The Premium edition is best for midsize and larger organizations at a higher price point with many additional capabilities on top of what is included in the Base edition. There are additional complimentary licenses to SAP BTP, more finance entitlements, SAP Analytics Cloud Planning to support extended planning and analysis activities, and both SAP Sales Cloud and Concur Expense Professional to further support sourcing and procurement activities.

Both the Base and Premium editions provide customers with CPEA credits that can be used to consume eligible services on SAP BTP, entitlements to SAP Build functionality to create apps, automate processes, and design business sites. The CPEA credits provided to each customer vary, as they are based on the **annual contract valuation (ACV)** of each unique contract.

Extensibility framework with GROW with SAP

Extensibility, the ability to extend and customize software, is a crucial feature demanded by customers. It enables them to tailor their business processes for competitive differentiation and allows partners to offer specialized industry functions or localization packages to meet global business needs.

Offering the capability for software extensions is essential, yet the approach to how these extensions are integrated is of equal importance. If the framework for adding extensions is flawed, it can detract from the added value that extensions are intended to provide. The extensibility framework of SAP S/4HANA Cloud has been carefully crafted, adhering to a set of design principles aimed at maximizing value:

- Ensures all customers begin with a standard, common foundation, which is crucial for maintaining consistency across different users' systems.
- Allows for the gradual expansion of features, ensuring that any enhancements are compatible with the core system, and preserving the initial common base.
- Facilitates easy customization by both partners and customers, making the software flexible and adaptable to a wide range of business needs.
- Embraces a comprehensive array of adaptation methods, providing flexibility for various types of customizations and extensions required by different businesses.

Extension can be implemented in two different approaches:

Side-by-side extensibility employs the full suite of features offered by a **Platform-as-a-Service** (**PaaS**) platform, leveraging a wider range of tools and services for comprehensive customization.

Side-by-side extensibility is particularly valuable for creating entirely new user interfaces that adhere to the SAP Fiori design principles or for integrating seamlessly with other SAP applications. This approach allows for the development of fresh applications and business processes that operate directly on the SAP Business Technology Platform, maintaining a loose coupling with the backend ABAP platform of SAP S/4HANA or other SAP solutions.

Key user (In-App) extensibility, on the other hand, is executed directly within the software stack itself, allowing for more immediate and integrated customizations.

For on-premise SAP S/4HANA deployments, both key user and side-by-side extensibility methods are accessible. However, these environments also support classic extensibility, which offers the full range of customization through ABAP coding via the ABAP in Eclipse **integrated development environment** (**IDE**). This provides developers with the most extensive flexibility to tailor and extend the functionality of SAP systems.

The concept of side-by-side extensibility, as through the SAP Business Technology Platform (as shown in the following figure), is rooted in the objective of cultivating a cloud-centric approach and leveraging cloud-native protocols to the fullest extent.

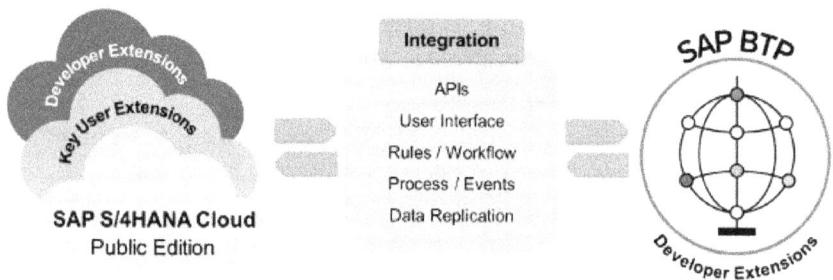

Figure 2.5: Side by side extensions

This strategic move empowers SAP clients to incorporate modular applications seamlessly, thereby augmenting their existing business processes and devising new ones beyond the scope of the standard software offerings. By adopting this method, SAP customers can create distinctive solutions that set them apart from competitors, providing a platform for innovation that can lead to considerable competitive benefits. This extensibility not only offers flexibility in customization but also aligns with the agility and scalability inherent in cloud environments, enabling businesses to swiftly adapt to market changes and evolving industry demands.

When creating side-by-side extensions, developers need to consider numerous integration areas. Specifically, within the user interface realm, they have the capability to insert tiles into the SAP Business Technology Platform Launchpad Service. These tiles serve as links to applications running on an S/4HANA system. Moreover, dynamic rebranding enables the incorporation of a customer's unique colors and trademarks directly into their corporate portal.

Within the domain of user management, developers have the ability to implement authentication and authorization processes through the SAP Business Technology Platform Identity Authentication Service.

Regarding rules and workflows, developers are equipped to leverage the SAP Business Technology Platform Business Rules Service as well as the SAP Business Technology Platform Workflow Management.

In the area of process integration, developers can employ the Cloud Connector in conjunction with the SAP Business Technology Platform Connectivity Service. This combination is used to establish SSL Tunnels, ensuring the secure transmission of data. Additionally, the SAP Business Technology Platform Destination Service is useful for maintaining information about various backend systems, encompassing both cloud and on-premise solutions, within the system infrastructure. For the creation of custom APIs, developers can utilize the SAP Business Technology Platform API Management Service.

Within the realm of event management, the SAP Business Technology Platform Event Mesh Service, previously referred to as Enterprise Messaging, can be deployed to enable asynchronous event-based communication among applications.

In the sphere of data integration, developers can utilize the SAP Business Technology Platform SAP HANA Cloud Service for managing standalone databases. Additionally, the SAP Business Technology Platform Cloud Integration for Data Services is available for integrating data between on-premise systems and cloud environments, employing a scheduled (batch) approach.

SAP has introduced a range of APIs for its SAP S/4HANA Cloud and other cloud-based products. These APIs facilitate the digital transformation of businesses by allowing secure integration of applications with different systems. Available through the SAP API Business Hub, these APIs include options for oData/REST and SOAP protocols.

Additionally, SAP has launched **Core Data Services (CDS)** views for SAP S/4HANA Cloud. These views are instrumental in accessing data from the SAP S/4HANA Cloud system. They can be utilized as oData services, made possible through tailor-made communication arrangements. This development enhances the extensibility and interoperability of SAP's cloud offerings, providing users with more flexibility in managing and analyzing their data.

In the realm of constructing parallel extensions on the SAP Business Technology Platform, developers have two distinct approaches to choose from. These are the SAP **Cloud Application Programming Model (CAP)** and the ABAP **RESTful Application Programming Model (RAP)**.

The CAP model employs open-source programming languages such as JAVA or Python, which correspondingly operate on their respective runtimes, like the JVM for JAVA. In contrast, RAP applications utilize ABAP as their programming language and function within the ABAP Environment of the SAP Business Technology Platform.

Both the CAP and RAP models support the development of applications optimized for SAP HANA. They are grounded in Core Data Services Technology, albeit with minor variations between the two. This technology framework assists developers in crafting data models and service models with semantic depth, based on the OData specification. These OData services are then instrumental in the development of SAP Fiori Applications.

Selecting the right programming model in application development is not a uniform process. Both CAP and RAP can effectively address numerous scenarios. However, as a developer, there are several aspects to weigh in your decision-making. Primarily, your expertise plays a crucial role. If you are proficient in JAVA or Python, leveraging these skills is practical, especially under tight deadlines that do not allow for learning new languages. The nature of the systems within your infrastructure also matters. Moreover, once you have clarity on specific scenarios and use cases, a particular model might show a clear advantage. For instance, in situations involving the custom development of an OData API sourced from SAP S/4HANA Cloud, RAP might offer a more streamlined approach. It is vital to evaluate each scenario independently to choose the most suitable model.

The ABAP RAP Model is an advanced framework specifically tailored for the efficient creation of SAP HANA-optimized OData services, which are integral to Fiori applications. This model is adept at facilitating the development of diverse Fiori apps and the publication of Web APIs. It utilizes CDS for establishing data models with deep semantic layers and employs a service model infrastructure designed for crafting OData services. These services are intricately linked to an OData protocol and are supported by ABAP-based application services for bespoke logic and SAPUI5-based interfaces.

Integrating these capabilities into the SAP Business Technology Platform enhances the synergy between ABAP and cloud-native technologies, thereby enriching the scope of development projects. This integration allows for the creation and management of development artifacts directly in the cloud. It offers streamlined, end-to-end lifecycle management within a single ecosystem. The SAP BTP ABAP Environment ensures that everything from the ABAP Platform version to the SAP HANA Service is current and regularly updated. Moreover, with the SAP BTP ABAP Environment operating in the cloud, SAP handles operational aspects, enabling developers to focus on tasks that add more value.

The Extensibility for SAP S/4HANA Cloud provides a robust framework to help shape and hone your strategy for extensions. Customers are encouraged to begin with the SAP Best Practice Explorer, a comprehensive resource for discovering, exploring, and adopting best practices offered by SAP and its partners. This platform features an intuitive interface for seamless navigation. It organizes content into well-defined solution packages linked to specific products, which users can filter by industry sector, technology type, cloud specifics, or S/4HANA capabilities. An alphabetical search function is also provided to facilitate quick retrieval. Each package contains a central start page and a suite of additional materials, including software and delivery prerequisites, as well as configuration guides, all arranged systematically within folders.

The SAP Extensibility Explorer offers customers access to a comprehensive collection of more than twenty different scenarios, encompassing a vast array of extension types, both In-App and side-by-side, catering to nearly all possible needs. These scenarios can be conveniently sifted through by technology type. Each scenario is detailed with a description, key features, a diagrammatic representation of the development workflow, involved technologies, necessary preconditions, and pertinent APIs and services.

Additionally, SAP GROW also offers In-App extensibility. The comprehensive extensibility options are shown as follows:

	In-App Extensibility		
	Key User Extensibility	**Developer Extensibility**	**Side-by-Side Extensibility**
Scenario	Smaller low/no code extensions	Tightly-coupled, more complex extensions & apps	Loosely-coupled extensions & apps
Use Cases	• Custom fields, change UI field layout, forms and templates • Custom business objects or logic • Custom analytics via CDS views	• Extensions of released SAP objects • Partner extensions • Custom apps	• Industry cloud partner apps • Custom apps using ABAP or non-ABAP (Java, Java Script, Python, etc.)
Role	Key User	ABAP Developer	Developer
Benefit	• Fully managed and integrated in SAP S/4HANA Cloud • No coding skills needed	• Extend released SAP objects • More development options than key user extensibility	• Decoupled extensions are independent of SAP S/4HANA Cloud system & upgrade cycles
Environment	SAP S/4HANA Cloud, Public Edition		SAP Business Technology Platform

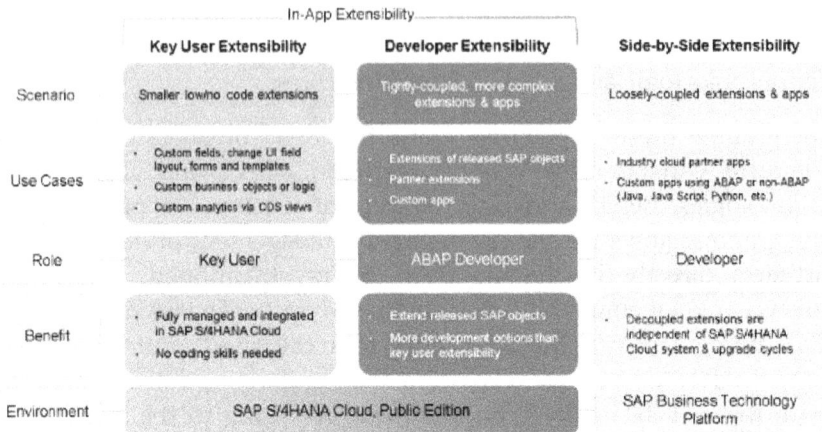

Figure 2.6: SAP Extensibility options

Additional components

In today's rapidly evolving business landscape, organizations require more than just a robust ERP system to maintain their competitive edge. Recognizing this need, SAP has thoughtfully curated comprehensive enablement packages through RISE and GROW with SAP that extend far beyond traditional ERP functionality. These packages encompass a rich ecosystem of tools and capabilities designed to address the modern enterprise's needs for extension, integration, automation, advanced analytics, and sustainability.

Empowering business innovation through low-code/no-code solutions

At the heart of SAP's extension strategy lies SAP Build, a revolutionary suite of low-code/no-code tools that democratizes application development and process automation. This powerful platform consists of three core components: SAP Build Apps, SAP Build Process Automation, and SAP Build Work Zone.

SAP Build Apps represents a paradigm shift in application development, enabling both technical and non-technical users to create sophisticated business applications through an intuitive drag-and-drop interface. This democratization of development allows organizations to rapidly respond to business needs without being constrained by traditional development cycles or technical resource limitations.

Complementing this capability, SAP Build Process Automation brings the power of workflow automation and **robotic process automation (RPA)** into the hands of business users. By combining these capabilities with embedded AI, organizations can streamline their operations and eliminate repetitive tasks while ensuring process consistency and compliance.

The SAP Build Work Zone serves as the digital workplace hub, allowing organizations to create engaging business sites that provide centralized access to applications, processes, and information. This unified approach to workplace technology ensures that employees, partners, and customers can easily access the tools and information they need, whether on desktop or mobile devices.

Enabling the modern workforce

Understanding the increasingly mobile nature of today's workforce, SAP has developed SAP Mobile Start, a native mobile application that brings the power of SAP solutions to iOS and Android devices. This app serves as a personalized gateway to business applications and data, featuring intelligent notifications and widgets that enable quick actions on the go. When integrated with SAP Task Center as depicted below, it provides a unified view of workflow tasks across different applications, ensuring business continuity regardless of location.

Figure 2.7: SAP Mobile workforce

Financial excellence and integration

The advanced financial management capabilities (as depicted below) included in RISE and GROW with SAP address the complex needs of modern financial operations. From group reporting and consolidation to cash management and receivables management, these tools enable organizations to maintain financial accuracy while accelerating their closing processes.

Figure 2.8: Advanced financial management

Intelligent spend and supplier collaboration

The **Intelligent Spend Business Network (ISBN)** components provide a comprehensive suite of tools for managing procurement and supplier relationships. The SAP Business Network Supplier Portal streamlines supplier collaboration and compliance, while Ariba Buying provides an intuitive procurement experience. The addition of central invoice management and its inbound processing module ensures efficient and accurate invoice processing across the organization.

Customer engagement and experience

SAP Sales Cloud V2 delivers a unified approach to customer relationship management, combining sales automation with enhanced retail execution capabilities. This integration provides organizations with complete visibility into their sales processes, enabling improved win rates and revenue growth. The inclusion of Concur Expense Professional further streamlines expense management, providing a comprehensive view of employee spending.

Artificial intelligence and analytics

The introduction of SAP Joule represents a significant leap forward in business AI capabilities. This digital assistant combines artificial intelligence with business context to help users navigate applications, provide support, and surface relevant information. Complementing this are AI Units that can be applied to various AI services, allowing organizations to leverage artificial intelligence where it provides the most value.

SAP Analytics Cloud Planning and SAP Datasphere provide the analytical foundation needed for data-driven decision-making. While Analytics Cloud Planning enables collaborative planning and forecasting, Datasphere creates a unified data fabric across SAP and non-SAP sources, ensuring that organizations can leverage all their data assets effectively.

Sustainability leadership

For organizations utilizing the private cloud edition, SAP's sustainability solutions provide comprehensive capabilities for managing **Environmental, Social, and Governance (ESG)** initiatives. SAP Sustainability Control Tower enables the collection and analysis of ESG data, while Sustainability Footprint Management provides detailed insights into carbon footprint across the value chain.

Flexible infrastructure and integration

The CPEA credits, as depicted in *Figure 2.7*, provide the flexibility organizations need to explore and implement various SAP Business Technology Platform services. This consumption-based model allows organizations to adapt their technology stack as their needs evolve, ensuring they can always access the capabilities they need while maintaining cost control.

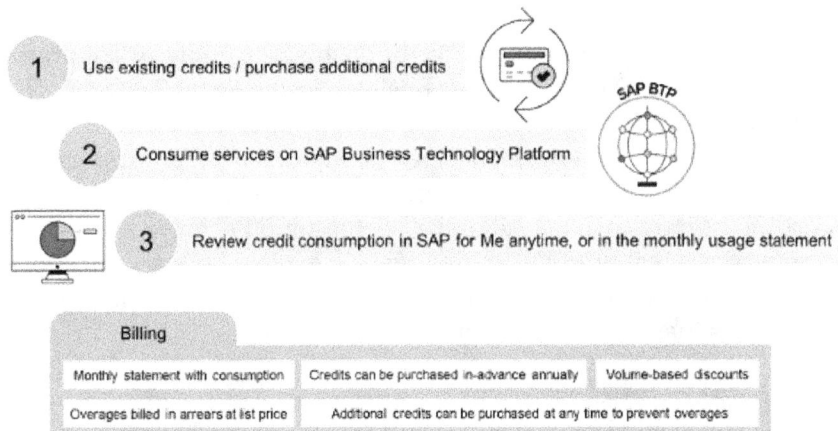

Figure 2.9: SAP CPEA, purchasing credits

Conclusion

In conclusion, the evolution of SAP deployment models from the traditional perpetual licensing to the more dynamic and flexible subscription-based models, such as RISE with SAP and GROW with SAP, marks a significant transformation in how enterprises approach ERP systems. This shift not only reflects changes in technological capabilities but also aligns with the broader industry trends toward cloud services and agile software development.

Through the exploration of different deployment environments, traditional SAP S/4HANA versus the cloud-based RISE with SAP and GROW with SAP, this chapter has highlighted the critical differences and benefits that these modern approaches offer. Access to innovative build capabilities, along with changes in the methods of development, configuration change management, and code deployment, shows a clear shift towards more efficient and scalable ERP solutions. The comparative analysis of tooling across the RISE, GROW, and native SAP S/4HANA environments further illustrates the choices organizations must consider to optimize their systems effectively.

As SAP continues to evolve, the importance of understanding these deployment options and the associated developmental methodologies and tools becomes paramount. Organizations that adeptly navigate these choices will likely gain significant competitive advantages, leveraging the full potential of SAP solutions to meet their unique business needs. Thus, the journey of SAP deployment is not only about technological adoption but also about strategic business transformation.

Building on these foundational components, our journey continues into the expansive world of SAP Business Technology Platform. The next chapter unravels the platform's comprehensive suite of services, examining how its key pillars, Data and Analytics, Application Development, Automation, Integration, and Artificial Intelligence, work in concert to drive digital transformation. Through practical examples and real-world scenarios, we will explore how organizations can harness these capabilities to create intelligent, integrated enterprises that are ready for tomorrow's challenges.

Multiple choice questions

1. **When was RISE with SAP introduced?**

    a. December 2020

    b. January 2021

    c. March 2021

    d. January 2022

2. **Which statement best describes the difference between RISE with SAP and GROW with SAP?**

    a. RISE is for cloud deployment, while GROW is for on-premises

    b. RISE offers a private cloud edition, while GROW focuses on a public cloud edition

    c. RISE is only for large enterprises, while GROW is for small businesses

    d. RISE is for technical services, while GROW is for business services

3. **What is the key financial benefit of moving to RISE with SAP?**

    a. Increased capital expenditure

    b. Higher maintenance costs

    c. Shift from CapEx to OpEx

    d. Reduced cloud costs

4. **What are the two main types of extensibilities available in SAP S/4HANA Cloud?**

    a. Internal and external extensions

    b. Side-by-side and In-App extensions

    c. Cloud and on-premises extensions

    d. Basic and advanced extensions

5. **Which component is included in the GROW with SAP Premium edition but not in the Base edition?**

    a. SAP Build Apps

    b. SAP Analytics Cloud Planning

    c. SAP BTP CPEA credits

    d. Ariba Buying

6. **What is the primary purpose of SAP Build in the context of RISE and GROW?**

   a. Infrastructure construction

   b. Low-code/no-code development

   c. Database building

   d. Network configuration

7. **What is a key characteristic of SAP's mobile strategy in RISE and GROW?**

   a. Limited to desktop applications

   b. Native mobile apps with SAP Mobile Start

   c. Web-only mobile access

   d. Third-party mobile solutions only

8. **Which financial management capability is available in RISE with SAP?**

   a. Basic accounting only

   b. Manual consolidation tools

   c. Group reporting and consolidation

   d. Local accounting only

9. **What role does SAP Joule play in the RISE and GROW offerings?**

   a. Database management

   b. Network configuration

   c. AI-powered digital assistance

   d. Hardware provisioning

10. **What is the significance of CPEA credits in the RISE and GROW packages?**

    a. They can only be used for storage

    b. They provide flexibility in consuming BTP services

    c. They are limited to development tools

    d. They can only be used for testing

Answers

1. b

   Explanation: RISE with SAP was unveiled in January 2021 as a comprehensive business transformation offering designed to help organizations transition to becoming intelligent enterprises through cloud adoption.

2. b

   Explanation: RISE with SAP primarily offers SAP S/4HANA Cloud, private edition, providing more customization flexibility, while GROW with SAP focuses on the public cloud edition with standardized processes and continuous innovation.

3. c

   Explanation: RISE with SAP enables organizations to shift their IT investments from CapEx to OpEx, providing more predictable spending and better budgeting capabilities.

4. b

   Explanation: SAP S/4HANA Cloud supports two primary types of extensibility: side-by-side extensions (using SAP BTP) and In-App extensions (key user extensibility), allowing different approaches to customizing and extending functionality.

5. b

   Explanation: SAP Analytics Cloud Planning is included specifically in the Premium edition of GROW with SAP, providing extended planning and analysis capabilities not available in the Base edition.

6. b

   Explanation: SAP Build provides low-code/no-code development capabilities, enabling both technical and business users to create applications, automate processes, and design business sites without extensive coding knowledge.

7. b

   Explanation: SAP Mobile Start provides native mobile applications for iOS and Android devices, offering personalized access to business applications and data with intelligent notifications and widgets.

8. c

Explanation: RISE with SAP includes advanced financial management capabilities such as group reporting and consolidation, enabling organizations to maintain financial accuracy and accelerate closing processes.

9. c

Explanation: SAP Joule is an AI-powered digital assistant that combines artificial intelligence with business context to help users navigate applications, provide support, and surface relevant information.

10. b

Explanation: CPEA credits provide organizations with the flexibility to explore and implement various SAP Business Technology Platform services based on their needs, allowing for the adaptation of their technology stack as requirements evolve.

Join our book's Discord space

Join the book's Discord Workspace for Latest updates, Offers, Tech happenings around the world, New Release and Sessions with the Authors:

https://discord.bpbonline.com

CHAPTER 3

SAP Business Technology Platform and Cloud Provider Integration

Introduction

In today's rapidly evolving digital landscape, businesses are increasingly turning to cloud-based solutions to drive innovation, scalability, and efficiency. This chapter explores the powerful combination of SAP **Business Technology Platform (BTP)** and cloud provider integration, providing a comprehensive overview of how these technologies work together to enable digital transformation and empower organizations to thrive in the age of Industry 4.0. We will delve into the core components of SAP BTP, examine the importance of cloud provider integration, and explore real-world applications across various domains, including data management, application development, and advanced analytics.

Structure

The topics to be covered in the chapter are as follows:

- SAP Business Technology Platform
- Cloud provider integration

- Data and analytics
- Apps and API's
- Process Integration
- Machine learning

Objectives

By the end of this chapter, readers will understand the core components and capabilities of the SAP **Business Technology Platform** (**BTP**), recognize the importance of cloud provider integration in modern enterprise architecture, and explore real-world use cases demonstrating the synergy between SAP BTP and cloud providers, with a focus on AWS integration. They will also gain insights into the implementation of data lakes, data mesh, and machine learning solutions, and appreciate the role of SAP BTP and cloud provider integration in driving digital transformation. The chapter will also help understand the basics of AI Core and Generative AI Hub from SAP and be prepared for the next chapter on designing and building well-architected applications

It is important to note that the SAP BTP is a rapidly evolving ecosystem. The information provided in this chapter is current at the time of writing. However, given the dynamic nature of cloud technologies and SAP's continuous innovation, readers are strongly encouraged to refer to the latest SAP documentation for the most up-to-date and specific information on BTP services and capabilities.

This chapter places particular emphasis on use cases involving cloud provider integration, with a focus on **Amazon Web Services** (**AWS**). While the principles discussed can often be applied to other cloud providers, the examples and implementations are primarily centered around AWS to provide concrete and practical insights.

SAP Business Technology Platform

SAP BTP is SAP's comprehensive platform-as-a-service offering. It brings cloud capabilities for application development, automation, integration, data and analytics, and AI together in one unified environment. Optimized for and deeply integrated with SAP applications, SAP BTP provides customers, partners, and internal SAP teams with business-centric tools and content to enhance business processes and infuse intelligence in and beyond SAP-led enterprise landscapes.

The key aspects of SAP BTP are as follows:

- **Unified technology foundation:** SAP BTP is at the center of SAP's technology strategy, helping SAP development teams build applications and business capabilities in a unified way. It also enables SAP's suite qualities that foster technical integration and a harmonized user experience across applications.

- **Empowering innovation:** SAP BTP offers a well-curated set of commercial products and services that give customers and partners the opportunity to build and run new cloud applications in the same way as solutions built and operated by SAP. It also helps create unprecedented insights and innovation on top of and across SAP applications and third-party solutions.

- **AI capabilities:** To harness the power of generative **artificial intelligence (AI)**, SAP BTP provides prebuilt AI services for recurring business scenarios as well as tools to manage data, build intelligent applications, and manage their lifecycle effectively. It also gives trusted access to general-purpose AI technology from leading vendors, including various **large language models (LLMs)**.

- **Partner ecosystem:** For SAP partners, especially independent software vendors, SAP BTP is the go-to platform to develop and run solutions that augment the existing SAP product portfolio and offer it to joint customers through SAP's commercial channels, such as SAP Store.

Business perspective of SAP BTP

SAP BTP stands out due to its business-oriented approach, reflected in three key qualities:

- **Always-on business context:**
  - Enables access to semantically enriched data across the SAP portfolio
  - Preserves and enriches business context through various capabilities
  - Plans to build its own foundation model for creating SAP-specific AI use cases

- **Accelerated business outcomes**:
  o Provides free access to prebuilt business accelerators for recurring scenarios
  o Offers SAP Discovery Center missions to help users achieve results quickly
  o Includes simplified administration, one-click deployment, and AI-powered support
- **Business-friendly experience**:
  o Makes technology intuitive and easy to use
  o Embeds technology capabilities directly into the application experience
  o Empowers users with no-code editors, "drag and drop" features, and intelligent advisors
  o Integrates the AI copilot Joule across various SAP BTP services

Digital transformation and SAP BTP

SAP BTP plays a crucial role in addressing key challenges of digital transformation. Let us explore each of these challenges in detail:

- **Modernizing mature and sophisticated IT landscapes:** Many organizations have invested heavily in complex, on-premises IT systems over the years. These systems, while robust, often struggle to keep pace with the rapidly evolving digital landscape. SAP BTP provides a bridge between these legacy systems and modern cloud-based solutions, allowing for gradual modernization without disrupting critical business processes.
  o **Example**: A global manufacturing company, GlobeTech Industries, has been using SAP ECC for over 15 years. With SAP BTP, they are able to extend their core ERP functionality with cloud-based applications. For instance, they have implemented a mobile app for field service technicians built on SAP Build, which integrates seamlessly with their existing SAP ECC system. This allows them to modernize their field service operations without immediately replacing their entire ERP system.

- **Connecting processes across heterogeneous IT landscapes:** In today's business environment, companies often use a mix of solutions from various vendors, leading to siloed data and disconnected processes. SAP BTP provides robust integration capabilities that allow these disparate systems to work together seamlessly, creating a unified business process landscape.

  o **Example:** RetailGiant, a multi-national retail corporation, uses SAP S/4HANA for its core operations, Salesforce for CRM, and a custom-built inventory management system. Using SAP Integration Suite (part of SAP BTP), they have created an end-to-end order fulfillment process that spans all three systems. When a sale is made in Salesforce, it automatically triggers inventory checks in the custom system and creates the necessary transactions in SAP S/4HANA, ensuring a smooth, integrated process from sale to delivery.

- **Unleashing the power of data for better decision-making:** With the explosion of data from various sources, organizations often struggle to derive meaningful insights. SAP BTP provides powerful data management and analytics capabilities that allow businesses to consolidate, analyze, and visualize data from multiple sources, enabling data-driven decision-making.

  o **Example:** AgriCorp, a large agricultural products company, collects data from various sources, including IoT sensors in fields, weather stations, and market price feeds. Using SAP Datasphere and SAP Analytics Cloud (both part of SAP BTP), they have created a comprehensive analytics dashboard. This dashboard combines all these data sources to provide real-time insights on crop health, predicted yields, and optimal harvest times, allowing farm managers to make informed decisions that maximize crop output and profitability.

- **Accelerating agile and AI-powered innovation with limited resources:** In the fast-paced digital economy, businesses need to innovate quickly to stay competitive. However, many organizations face resource constraints, especially in terms of specialized IT skills. SAP BTP provides low-code/no-code development platforms and pre-built AI services that allow businesses to rapidly develop and deploy innovative solutions without extensive technical expertise.

    o **Example**: MediCare Solutions, a healthcare services provider, wanted to improve patient engagement but lacked the resources for a full-scale custom development project. Using SAP Build Apps and SAP AI Business Services (part of SAP BTP), they quickly developed a patient engagement app with an AI-powered chatbot. The app allows patients to schedule appointments, access their medical records, and get instant responses to common queries through the chatbot. This solution was developed in a fraction of the time and cost of traditional development, allowing MediCare to innovate rapidly despite limited IT resources.

By addressing these key challenges, SAP BTP enables businesses to navigate their digital transformation journey effectively. It provides the tools and capabilities needed to modernize IT landscapes, integrate disparate systems, harness the power of data, and drive innovation, all while optimizing resource utilization. Through SAP BTP, organizations can build the agile, data-driven, and intelligent enterprise needed to thrive in the digital age.

Consumption patterns

SAP BTP offers a variety of service types to cater to different business needs and technical requirements. The two primary categories of services are:

- **Software as a Service (SaaS):** SaaS offerings on SAP BTP provide ready-to-use applications and solutions that are fully managed by SAP. These services allow customers to quickly adopt and benefit from specific functionalities without the need for extensive setup or maintenance.

    o Key characteristics of SaaS offerings include:

    - Immediate availability and quick time-to-value

    - Regular updates and innovations managed by SAP

    - Scalability and flexibility to meet changing business needs

    - Reduced IT overhead and maintenance costs

o Examples of SaaS offerings on SAP BTP include SAP Analytics Cloud, SAP Datasphere, and SAP Build Process Automation.

- **Infrastructure as a Platform as a Service (iPaaS):** iPaaS offerings on SAP BTP provide a comprehensive set of tools and services that enable customers to build, integrate, and extend applications. These services offer more flexibility and control compared to SaaS offerings, allowing for customization and development of tailored solutions.

  o Key characteristics of iPaaS offerings include:

    ▪ Flexibility to build custom applications and extensions

    ▪ Integration capabilities with both SAP and non-SAP systems

    ▪ Access to development tools, frameworks, and runtime environments

    ▪ Support for various programming languages and development approaches

  o Examples of iPaaS offerings on SAP BTP include SAP Integration Suite, SAP HANA Cloud, SAP Business Application Studio, and the Cloud Foundry environment.

The combination of SaaS and iPaaS offerings within SAP BTP allows organizations to choose the right mix of services to meet their specific needs, whether it is rapid adoption of pre-built solutions or development of custom applications and integrations. The iPaaS offerings, in particular, provide the tools and platforms necessary for businesses to create tailored integration solutions and extend their SAP and non-SAP landscapes effectively.

Technology pillars in SAP BTP

SAP BTP is structured around five core pillars, each addressing key aspects of modern enterprise technology needs. Let us explore each pillar and its associated products in detail:

- **Application development:** Application development capabilities in SAP BTP enable organizations to create, extend, and customize applications to meet their specific business needs. This pillar includes:

o **SAP Build:** SAP Build is a low-code/no-code development platform that empowers both professional developers and citizen developers to create applications quickly and efficiently. It provides:

- Drag-and-drop interfaces for building user-friendly applications

- Pre-built templates and components to accelerate development

- Integration with SAP and non-SAP systems

- Collaboration tools for team-based development

o **SAP Build Code:** SAP Build Code is an AI-powered development environment for professional developers working with Java and JavaScript. Key features include:

- Intelligent code completion and suggestions

- Automated code refactoring and optimization

- Integration with popular development tools and frameworks

- Built-in testing and debugging capabilities

o **SAP BTP ABAP Environment:** The ABAP environment in SAP BTP allows organizations to develop and run ABAP applications in the cloud. It offers:

- Cloud-optimized ABAP development tools

- Seamless integration with SAP S/4HANA and other SAP solutions

- Support for modern ABAP programming models like RAP (RESTful ABAP Programming Model)

- Easy deployment and scalability in the cloud

- **Automation:** Automation capabilities in SAP BTP help organizations streamline their business processes and increase operational efficiency.

o **SAP Build Process Automation:** This solution combines **robotic process automation (RPA)**, artificial intelligence, and workflow management to automate complex business processes. It provides:

- Visual process modeling and automation design

- AI-powered document processing and data extraction
- Integration with SAP and non-SAP applications
- Monitoring and analytics for process optimization

- **Integration:** Integration capabilities allow organizations to connect various systems, applications, and data sources seamlessly.

  o **SAP Integration Suite:** SAP Integration Suite is a comprehensive **Integration Platform as a Service (iPaaS)** solution that enables organizations to connect applications, processes, and data across landscapes. It includes:

    - Pre-built integration content and adapters
    - API management and microservices support
    - B2B integration capabilities
    - Integration flow designer with AI-assisted development
    - Monitoring and analytics for integration scenarios

- **Data and analytics:** This pillar focuses on helping organizations manage, analyze, and derive insights from their data.

  o **SAP Analytics Cloud:** SAP Analytics Cloud is a SaaS solution that combines business intelligence, augmented analytics, and collaborative enterprise planning. Features include:

    - Interactive dashboards and data visualizations
    - Predictive analytics and forecasting
    - Collaborative planning and budgeting tools
    - Natural language query capabilities
    - Mobile analytics for on-the-go insights

  o **SAP Datasphere:** SAP Datasphere (formerly SAP Data Warehouse Cloud) is a comprehensive data management and analytics solution that provides:

    - Data integration and harmonization across multiple sources
    - Semantic layer for consistent business definitions
    - Data modeling and preparation tools
    - Built-in data quality and governance features

- Integration with SAP Analytics Cloud for seamless analysis

  o **SAP HANA Cloud:** SAP HANA Cloud is a cloud-native in-memory database that offers:

    - High-performance data processing and analytics

    - Support for structured and unstructured data

    - Advanced data processing capabilities like spatial and graph processing

    - Built-in application server for developing data-intensive applications

    - Scalability and flexibility in the cloud

- **Artificial intelligence:** The AI pillar focuses on bringing intelligent capabilities to business processes and applications.

  o **SAP AI Business Services:** These are pre-built AI services that can be easily integrated into business applications. They include:

    - Document classification and information extraction

    - Conversational AI for building chatbots and virtual assistants

    - Business entity recognition for automated data extraction

    - Personalized recommendation services

  o **Generative AI Hub:** The Generative AI Hub is a platform for developing and deploying Generative AI solutions within the SAP ecosystem. It offers:

    - Access to pre-trained large language models

    - Tools for fine-tuning models on domain-specific data

    - Integration capabilities with SAP applications

    - Governance and security features for responsible AI use

These five pillars and their associated products form the foundation of the SAP BTP, providing a comprehensive suite of tools and services for organizations to innovate, integrate, and transform their business processes in the digital age. By leveraging these capabilities, businesses can create intelligent, connected enterprises that are agile, data-driven, and ready for future challenges. This visualization demonstrates how these pillars work together to create a unified platform for digital transformation:

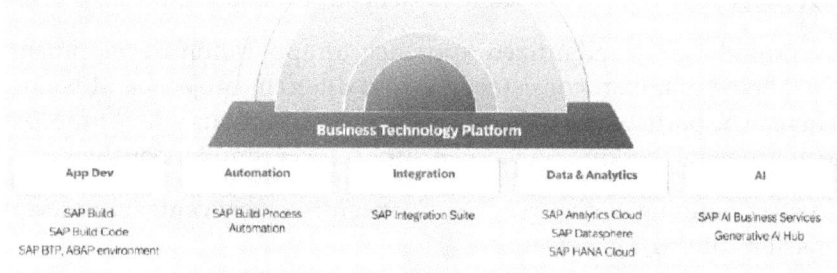

App Dev	Automation	Integration	Data & Analytics	AI
SAP Build	SAP Build Process	SAP Integration Suite	SAP Analytics Cloud	SAP AI Business Services
SAP Build Code	Automation		SAP Datasphere	Generative AI Hub
SAP BTP, ABAP environment			SAP HANA Cloud	

Figure 3.1: *The technology pillars of SAP BTP*

Development frameworks

In the world of enterprise software development, one size rarely fits all. SAP recognizes this and offers a variety of development frameworks within its BTP. These frameworks cater to different programming models, developer skills, and project requirements. Let us explore each of these frameworks and understand how they can help you build, extend, and integrate applications efficiently.

SAP Cloud Application Programming model

Imagine you are tasked with building a new enterprise-grade application that needs to be scalable, maintainable, and quick to develop. This is where the SAP **Cloud Application Programming (CAP)** model shines. CAP provides a consistent end-to-end programming model that supports the rapid development of microservices and user interface applications.

With CAP, you are not starting from scratch. It offers out-of-the-box business functionality and best practices, allowing you to focus on your application's unique features rather than reinventing the wheel. CAP is designed with microservices in mind, enabling you to create modular and scalable applications that can grow with your business needs.

One of CAP's strengths is its support for polyglot development. Whether your team prefers JavaScript (Node.js) or Java, CAP has you covered. This flexibility extends to scalability as well - applications built with CAP can easily scale in cloud environments, ensuring your solution can handle increased loads as your user base grows.

By providing a standardized approach to application development, CAP helps maintain consistency across different projects and teams. This can be particularly valuable in large organizations where multiple teams may be working on various applications simultaneously.

To start building with CAP, visit **https://discovery-center.cloud.sap/missionCatalog/?search=cap.**

ABAP RESTful Application Programming model

For organizations with a strong ABAP background, the ABAP **RESTful Application Programming** (**RAP**) model offers a path to modernization without abandoning existing skills and investments. RAP is specifically designed for developing SAP Fiori apps and Web APIs in the ABAP environment.

RAP supports the development of both transactional and analytical apps, giving you the flexibility to create a wide range of solutions. It enables the creation of OData services based on SAP Gateway, allowing your ABAP applications to communicate effectively with other systems and services.

One of RAP's key strengths is its opinionated architecture, which promotes clean and well-structured code. This can significantly improve the maintainability of your applications over time. RAP applications can scale effectively within the ABAP environment, ensuring your solutions can grow as your business expands.

Perhaps most importantly, RAP provides a bridge between your existing ABAP investments and modern development practices. It allows for the modernization of existing ABAP applications with RESTful principles, helping you evolve your applications without a complete rewrite.

To explore RAP development, check out **https://discovery-center. cloud.sap/missionCatalog/?search=rap.**

SAP Build

In today's fast-paced business environment, sometimes you need to create applications quickly without extensive coding knowledge. This is where SAP Build comes in. SAP Build is a low-code/no-code development platform that empowers citizen developers and business users to create applications with minimal technical expertise.

SAP Build includes intuitive drag-and-drop interfaces for building user interfaces, making it easy to design attractive and functional apps. It also offers pre-built connectors and integrations with SAP and third-party systems, allowing you to easily connect your new applications with existing data sources and processes.

The SAP Build suite comprises three main components:

- SAP Build Apps for creating web and mobile applications
- SAP Build Process Automation for automating business processes
- SAP Build Work Zone for creating digital workplace solutions

One of the key benefits of SAP Build is its ability to democratize development. It puts the power of application creation in the hands of those who understand the business needs best. This can lead to more relevant, user-friendly applications and can significantly reduce the time from idea to implementation.

To start building with SAP Build, visit **https://discovery-center.cloud.sap/missionCatalog/?search=sap%20build**.

Kyma

In the world of cloud-native development, Kyma stands out as a powerful tool in the SAP BTP toolkit. Kyma is an open-source project that extends the capabilities of Kubernetes, providing a flexible and scalable environment for developing microservices and serverless functions.

With Kyma, you can build event-driven applications that respond dynamically to changes in your business environment. It provides robust API management capabilities, allowing you to securely expose and consume APIs across your application landscape.

One of Kyma's key strengths is its support for serverless computing. This allows you to run code in response to events without worrying about the underlying infrastructure, potentially reducing costs and improving scalability.

Kyma is particularly well-suited for extending SAP applications in a cloud-native way. It allows you to add new capabilities to your SAP systems without modifying the core, promoting a clean core strategy that can simplify upgrades and maintenance.

To explore Kyma's capabilities, check out **https://discovery-center. cloud.sap/missionCatalog/?search=kyma.**

Cloud Foundry Environment

The Cloud Foundry Environment in SAP BTP offers a polyglot **platform-as-a-service** (**PaaS**) that supports multiple programming languages and runtimes. This makes it an excellent choice for organizations with diverse development skills and existing codebases in various languages.

With Cloud Foundry, you can deploy cloud-native applications quickly and easily. It provides built-in services for databases, messaging, and more, allowing you to focus on your application logic rather than infrastructure management.

One of the key benefits of Cloud Foundry is its built-in auto-scaling capabilities. Your applications can automatically scale up or down based on demand, ensuring optimal performance and resource utilization. Additionally, the portability of Cloud Foundry applications means you can easily move them between different Cloud Foundry environments if needed.

Cloud Foundry is particularly well-suited for microservices architectures. It provides the tools and services needed to deploy, manage, and scale complex microservices-based applications effectively.

To get started with Cloud Foundry, visit **https://discovery-center. cloud.sap/missionCatalog/?search=cloud%20foundry**.

SAP Business Application Studio

Last but not least, let us talk about where all this development happens. SAP Business Application Studio is a powerful, cloud-based development environment that supports multiple development scenarios, including SAP Fiori, CAP, and mobile development.

Think of Business Application Studio as your virtual workbench in the cloud. It offers pre-configured dev spaces for different project types, allowing you to start coding quickly without spending time on setup. It integrates seamlessly with Git for source control management, supporting modern development workflows and team collaboration.

The cloud-based nature of Business Application Studio means you can access your development environment from anywhere and easily scale your resources as needed. It is designed to boost developer productivity with features like intelligent code completion and integrated debugging tools.

Perhaps most importantly, Business Application Studio is tightly integrated with other SAP BTP services and tools, providing a seamless development experience across the SAP ecosystem.

To explore SAP Business Application Studio, check out **https:// discovery-center.cloud.sap/missionCatalog/?search=business%20 application%20studio**.

By offering this diverse set of development frameworks, SAP BTP ensures that developers can work in their preferred environment while leveraging the platform's integration capabilities and business services. Whether you are building microservices, extending existing applications, or creating new solutions from scratch, SAP BTP provides the tools and frameworks to support your development needs.

Cloud provider integration

Digital transformation has become imperative for businesses across industries, especially in the context of integrating cloud provider environments with the ERP backbone. This transformation is about adopting new technologies and reimagining processes, business models, and customer experiences to stay competitive in the digital age. One of the key drivers of digital transformation is Industry 4.0, which emphasizes the convergence of digital technologies with traditional industrial processes to create **smart factories** and enable seamless connectivity across the value chain. Here are some of the areas in which cloud provider integration brings advantages in cost and scale:

- **Apps/API:** In the digital transformation era, applications and APIs are crucial in enabling connectivity, agility, and innovation. With the proliferation of cloud computing and microservices architecture, businesses can develop and deploy applications faster. APIs facilitate seamless integration between different systems, allowing data to flow freely across the organization and enabling the creation of new services and business models. By leveraging low-code/no-code platforms like SAP Build Apps, organizations can accelerate app development and empower business users to participate in the innovation process.

- **Data and analytics:** Data is often called the new currency in the digital economy. In digital transformation, organizations need to harness the power of data and analytics to gain actionable insights, drive informed decision-making, and enhance operational efficiency. Solutions like SAP HANA Cloud and SAP Analytics Cloud enable organizations to process and analyze vast amounts of data in real-time, providing valuable insights into customer behavior, market trends, and operational performance. By leveraging advanced analytics capabilities, businesses can optimize processes, identify new revenue opportunities, and stay ahead of the competition.

- **Internet of Things (IoT):** The IoT is revolutionizing industries by enabling the connectivity of physical devices and assets, transforming them into intelligent, data-generating endpoints. In digital transformation, IoT technologies play a crucial role in driving operational efficiency, predictive maintenance, and enhanced customer experiences. By deploying sensors, actuators, and connected devices, organizations can collect real-time data from their assets, monitor performance, and proactively address issues before they escalate. Integrating IoT data with ERP systems enables organizations to achieve end-to-end visibility across their operations, optimize resource utilization, and deliver personalized products and services to customers.

- **Machine learning:** Machine learning is a subset of AI that enables systems to learn from data and make predictions or decisions without being explicitly programmed. In the context of digital transformation, machine learning technologies empower organizations to unlock their data's value, automate repetitive tasks, and drive innovation. By leveraging machine learning algorithms, organizations can analyze vast amounts of data to uncover patterns, trends, and anomalies, enabling them to make more accurate predictions and optimize business processes. Integrating machine learning capabilities with ERP systems enables organizations to enhance decision-making, automate routine tasks, and deliver personalized experiences to customers.

In summary, integrating cloud providers with SAP ERP systems and SAP BTP offers significant advantages for businesses seeking to accelerate their digital transformation journey. From enhanced innovation and scalability to cost efficiency and security, cloud provider integration enables organizations to unlock new opportunities for growth, competitiveness, and agility in the digital economy. By embracing cloud provider technologies, businesses can position themselves for success in an increasingly interconnected and data-driven world.

Data and analytics

In today's data-driven world, organizations are constantly seeking ways to manage, store, and derive value from the vast amounts of data they generate and collect. Two concepts that have gained significant traction in recent years are data lakes and data mesh. These approaches offer different strategies for handling big data and analytics in modern enterprises, as outlined in the following section.

Introduction to data lakes

Data lakes serve as centralized repositories for storing vast amounts of raw, unstructured, and structured data from various sources within an organization. Unlike traditional data warehouses that impose structure and schema on data before ingestion, data lakes store data in its native format, allowing for flexible and scalable storage of diverse data types. By consolidating data in a single location, organizations can establish a **single source of truth** for all their data assets, facilitating easier access, analysis, and insights generation. Data lakes are designed to accommodate large volumes of data from sources such as transactional systems, IoT devices, social media feeds, and more, enabling organizations to capture and retain valuable data for future analysis and decision-making, as indicated in the following figure:

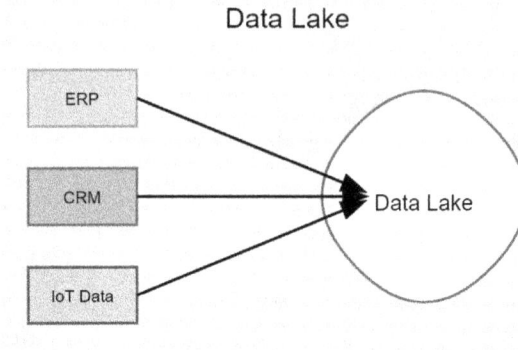

Figure 3.2: Data lake with replication

Introduction to data mesh

In contrast to data lakes, which centralize data storage and management, the data mesh approach decentralizes data management by distributing ownership and access across various source systems within the organization. In a data mesh architecture, each domain or business unit retains ownership of its data while exposing standardized interfaces for access and integration. This decentralized model empowers domain experts to manage and govern their data effectively while enabling seamless data sharing and collaboration across the organization. By adopting a data mesh strategy, as visually depicted below, organizations can leverage existing data infrastructure and avoid the pitfalls of centralization, such as data silos and scalability challenges.

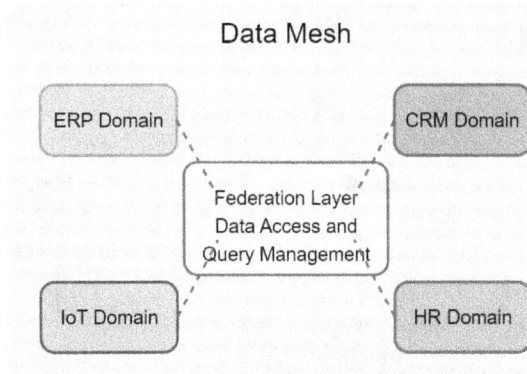

Figure 3.3: Data Mesh with Federation

Cloud providers integration- Data

SAP offers a range of solutions and technologies to support the implementation of data lakes within organizations, leveraging both on-premises and cloud-based architectures. With SAP Datasphere and SAP HANA Cloud, organizations can orchestrate the ingestion, processing, and analysis of large volumes of data from disparate sources, enabling them to derive actionable insights and drive informed decision-making. Additionally, SAP's integration with cloud provider platforms such as AWS, Microsoft Azure, and **Google Cloud Platform** (**GCP**) allows organizations to leverage scalable storage solutions, such as Amazon S3 or Google Cloud Storage, for building and managing their data lakes. By combining the capabilities of SAP and cloud provider technologies, organizations can unlock the full potential of their data assets, enabling them to drive innovation, improve operational efficiency, and gain a competitive edge in the digital marketplace.

In today's rapidly evolving business landscape, more than the traditional approach of relying solely on SAP BW as the single data warehouse is needed. With the proliferation of non-SAP systems, including devices, SaaS applications, and full-stack applications, organizations face an expanding and diverse data footprint. This necessitates a shift towards integrated data mesh or a single source of truth data lake solutions to meet the growing demands for analytics and machine learning.

Before looking at the specifics of cloud provider integration, let us revisit some of the key data and analytics solutions offered by SAP:

- **SAP Analytics Cloud**: SAP Analytics Cloud is a SaaS solution that combines business intelligence, augmented analytics, and collaborative enterprise planning.
- **SAP Datasphere:** SAP Datasphere (formerly SAP Data Warehouse Cloud) is a comprehensive data management and analytics solution.
- **SAP HANA Cloud**: SAP HANA Cloud is a cloud-native in-memory database.

Each of these solutions represents a cornerstone in the SAP ecosystem, combining sophisticated functionalities to address various data management and analytics needs. In the pre-BTP era, customers used SAP BW for reporting, SAP Data Services for ETL, and SAP BPC for planning. These functionalities are now consolidated within SAP Datasphere and SAP Analytics Cloud.

Now, let us explore the reference architecture for cloud provider integration:

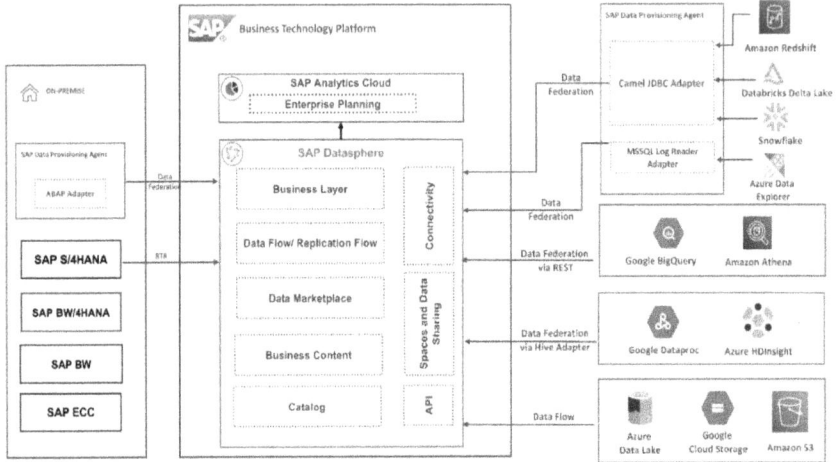

Figure 3.4: *SAP Data to value architecture*

Customers can harness the power of cloud provider platforms to augment their data management and analytics capabilities. By leveraging the data federation capabilities within SAP Datasphere, organizations can seamlessly combine SAP business data with data stored in popular cloud providers or SaaS offerings. This integration offers real-time access to SAP S/4HANA data, robust security, governance features, and self-service analytical capabilities through SAP Analytics Cloud.

Moreover, with the FedML library, data scientists can federate data required for machine learning experiments directly on cloud provider platforms in real-time. The bidirectional nature of data federation enables customers to choose between hosting their datamesh in cloud provider solutions or SAP Datasphere, depending on their specific requirements.

Additionally, organizations can schedule replication flows to cloud provider solutions like Amazon S3, ensuring data consistency and availability across platforms. Furthermore, leveraging data from SAP Datasphere for machine learning experiments enables organizations to bring back inferences and forecasts to create a unified semantic layer through data federation or replication. This seamless integration between SAP and cloud provider technologies empowers organizations to derive actionable insights and drive informed decision-making.

To explore these capabilities further, visit the SAP Discovery Center mission **https://discovery-center.cloud.sap/missionde-tail/3656/3699/?tab=overview**.

Apps and API's

The landscape of custom application development within SAP systems has undergone a remarkable transformation over the years. In the early days, developers primarily focused on creating custom transactions (t-codes), BSP/Webdynpro applications, or SAP Enterprise Portal developments. However, as technology rapidly evolved, bringing with it widespread browser adoption, virtualization, distributed computing, and the rise of SaaS, the approach to custom application development shifted dramatically.

Today's applications are built on microservices-based architectures, enabling decoupled and modular development that offers greater flexibility and scalability. This shift has given rise to the concept of a **clean core** - a modern approach to extending ERP functionality while maintaining a stable, upgrade-safe, and transparent core system. The clean core philosophy emphasizes separating core ERP functionalities from customizations and innovations, supported by governance and guidelines that ensure the ERP system remains flexible and ready for future enhancements.

To illustrate the benefits of this new approach, consider an aerospace repair and overhaul shop that receives **purchase orders** (**POs**) from customers in PDF format. In the past, a custom application built within the SAP system would handle this process, reading the PDF, creating the order, and sending communications via email. Now, by decoupling this process and building the custom application on the SAP BTP, the shop can integrate with cloud providers for scalable notifications, enhancing flexibility and simplifying integration.

This evolution in custom application development has also embraced serverless computing, also known as **Function as a Service** (**FaaS**). In this cloud computing model, the provider dynamically manages resource allocation, allowing developers to focus solely on writing code triggered by events like HTTP requests or database updates. The cloud provider handles infrastructure concerns, automatically scaling resources as needed, freeing developers from the complexities of server provisioning and management.

As we look at the clean core guiding principles, we see a structured approach to modernization that balances innovation with stability. These principles encourage developers to build extensions and customizations outside the core ERP system, leveraging platforms like SAP BTP to create modular, scalable solutions that can evolve independently of the core. This approach not only simplifies upgrades and maintenance but also accelerates innovation by allowing teams to adopt new technologies and methodologies without compromising the integrity of the core ERP system.

In essence, the evolution of custom application development in SAP ecosystems reflects a broader shift in the technology landscape towards more agile, scalable, and modular architectures. By embracing concepts like the clean core, decoupled applications, and serverless computing, organizations can now create more responsive, efficient, and future-proof solutions that drive business value while maintaining the stability and reliability of their core ERP systems. As indicated in the following figure, the guiding principles include decoupling extensions to SAP BTP and staying close to the standard ERP configuration as much as possible:

Clean Core on RISE with SAP, SAP BTP and AWS

Clean core guiding principles

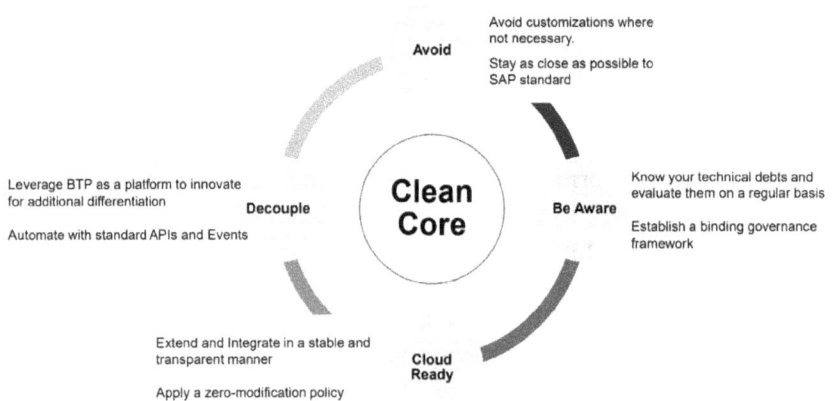

Avoid customizations where not necessary.

Avoid

Stay as close as possible to SAP standard

Leverage BTP as a platform to innovate for additional differentiation

Decouple

Automate with standard APIs and Events

Clean Core

Know your technical debts and evaluate them on a regular basis

Be Aware

Establish a binding governance framework

Extend and Integrate in a stable and transparent manner

Cloud Ready

Apply a zero-modification policy

Figure 3.5: Clean core guiding principles

The use cases and examples are as follows:

- **Use case 1, CAP application integration with Amazon SNS**: This use case involves integrating a CAP application with Amazon **Simple Notification Service (SNS)**. For instance, consider a scenario where business partner master data creation follows a process workflow, with notifications sent to the partner upon successful creation. As depicted in the following figure, a CAP application utilizes Amazon SNS to send bulk notifications, reducing cost and gaining scale efficiencies.

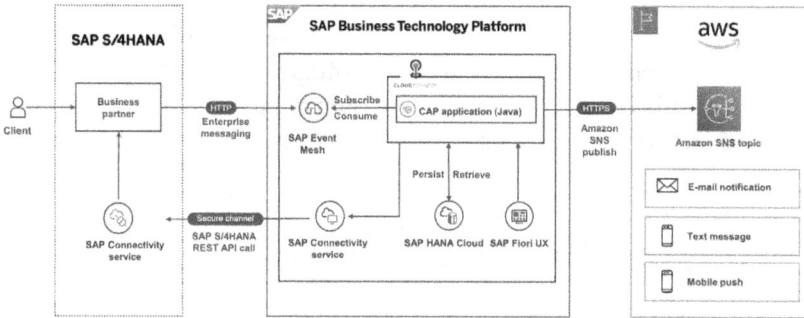

Figure 3.6:CAP application with Amazon SNS

Detailed instructions for executing this integration can be found in the provided GitHub repository: **https://open.sap. com/courses/aws1/overview**.

- **Use case 2, Enhance your business processes with SAP Build Process Automation**: SAP Build Process Automation offers low-code/no-code solutions for automating workflows, leveraging workflow management, **Robotic Process Automation (RPA)**, and AI capabilities. By enhancing business processes with automation, organizations can streamline operations, improve efficiency, and reduce manual effort. As depicted in the following figure, the build app consumes data from Amazon S3 via the Amazon API Gateway on a need basis:

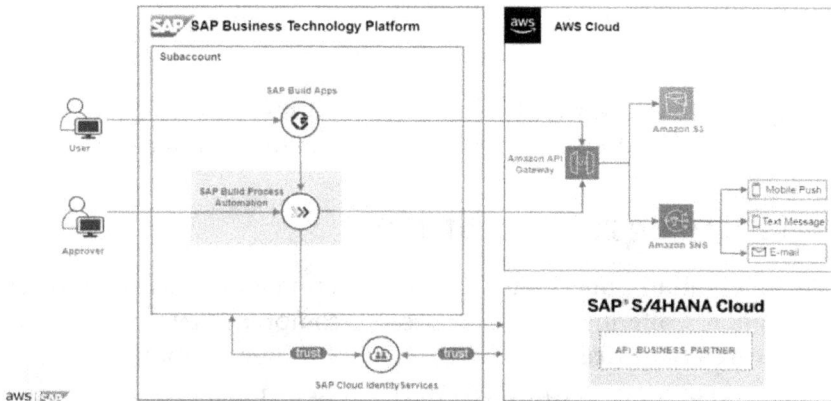

Figure 3.7: Build app with Amazon S3/SNS

For more hands-on examples, please visit https://discovery-center. cloud.sap/missionCatalog/?search=clean-core.

Process Integration

In today's interconnected business world, the ability to seamlessly integrate various systems, applications, and data sources is crucial for creating an intelligent enterprise. SAP Integration Suite stands at the forefront of this integration challenge, offering a comprehensive set of tools and capabilities to connect diverse landscapes, both within and beyond SAP ecosystems.

Understanding SAP Process Integration

SAP Process Integration is the cornerstone of SAP's integration strategy, encompassing various aspects of data and process connectivity. It enables the seamless exchange of information between different systems, applications, and services within an organization's IT landscape. This integration can occur through multiple channels:

- File transfers
- Shared databases
- APIs
- Connectors
- Messaging protocols
- Events
- Streaming
- Orchestration mechanisms

The goal is to create a unified, efficient, and responsive IT ecosystem that supports modern business processes and decision-making.

SAP Integration Suite

SAP Integration Suite builds upon the foundations of SAP Process Integration, offering a cloud-based, comprehensive integration **Platform as a Service (iPaaS)**. Let us study its key components:

- **Integration platform:** At the heart of SAP Integration Suite is a unified platform that covers multiple integration scenarios:

- o **Application-to-Application (A2A):** Connecting different software applications within an organization.

- o **Business-to-Business (B2B):** Facilitating communication between different organizations' systems.

- o **Business-to-Consumer (B2C):** Enabling interactions between business systems and consumer-facing applications.

- o **Machine-to-Machine (M2M):** Supporting communication between devices or systems without human intervention.

- o **Event-based integration:** Allowing systems to respond to real-time events.

- o **API-based integration:** Enabling applications to communicate through standardized interfaces.

This versatility ensures that organizations can handle virtually any integration scenario they encounter.

- **Connectivity:** SAP Integration Suite provides robust infrastructure and protocols for establishing connections between disparate systems. This includes:

  - o Pre-built adapters for SAP and non-SAP systems

  - o Support for various communication protocols (HTTP, HTTPS, FTP, SFTP, etc.)

  - o Cloud-to-cloud and cloud-to-on-premise integration capabilities

  - o Secure connectivity options, including VPN and reverse proxy

- **Orchestration:** The orchestration capabilities of SAP Integration Suite allow for the coordination and management of complex integration workflows. This includes:

  - o Visual flow designer for creating integration scenarios

  - o Support for both simple and complex routing logic

  - o Error handling and exception management

  - o Stateful and stateless process execution

- **Transformation:** Data rarely comes in a one-size-fits-all format. SAP Integration Suite offers powerful tools for transforming data formats, structures, and protocols:

- o Graphical mapping tools for complex transformations
- o Support for various data formats (XML, JSON, CSV, etc.)
- o Code-based transformation for advanced scenarios
- o Pre-built transformation templates for common use cases
- **Monitoring and analytics:** To ensure the smooth operation of integration processes, SAP Integration Suite provides comprehensive monitoring and analytics features:
  - o Real-time monitoring of integration flows
  - o Detailed logs and error tracking
  - o Performance analytics and bottleneck identification
  - o Customizable dashboards and alerts
- **API management:** In addition to the core integration capabilities, SAP Integration Suite includes robust API management features:
  - o API design and development tools
  - o API security and access control
  - o API analytics and monitoring
  - o Developer portal for API discovery and consumption
- **Integration assessment and advisory:** SAP Integration Suite goes beyond just providing tools. It also offers:
  - o Integration strategy assessment
  - o Best practice recommendations
  - o Integration pattern guidance
  - o Continuous improvement suggestions

Real-world impact

The power of the SAP Integration Suite lies in its ability to solve real-world integration challenges. For example:

- A global retailer used SAP Integration Suite to connect its e-commerce platform with its SAP S/4HANA backend, enabling real-time inventory updates and order processing.
- A manufacturing company leveraged the B2B capabilities of SAP Integration Suite to streamline its supply chain, connecting with suppliers and logistics partners for improved efficiency.

- A healthcare provider utilized the API management features to securely expose patient data to authorized third-party applications, enhancing patient care while maintaining data privacy.

By providing a comprehensive set of integration tools and capabilities, the SAP Integration Suite enables organizations to create connected, intelligent enterprises that can respond quickly to market changes and customer needs.

To explore SAP Integration Suite and start your integration journey, visit **https://discovery-center.cloud.sap/missionCatalog/?search=integration%20suite.**

Cloud providers

Integrating cloud provider solutions with SAP systems is crucial for realizing meaningful business outcomes and leveraging the full potential of enterprise data and processes. Here are some scenarios where such integration is beneficial:

- **Quality inspection enhancement**: Leveraging computer vision technology on cloud provider platforms can enhance quality inspection processes. For example, using Amazon SageMaker for image analysis can improve quality control in manufacturing operations, leading to higher customer satisfaction and reduced returns.

- **Predictive maintenance**: By integrating sensor data from industrial equipment with SAP systems, organizations can predict equipment failures and schedule maintenance proactively. This approach optimizes asset utilization and reduces operational costs by minimizing downtime.

- **Personalization in retail:** Retailers can enhance customer experiences by deploying machine learning models on cloud provider platforms to offer personalized product recommendations. This improves customer engagement and boosts sales revenue.

Use cases

Use cases with cloud provider solutions are as follows:

- **Use case 1:** Integrate Events from Amazon IoT services with SAP S/4HANA using SAP BTP:

  o Amazon Monitron detects abnormal conditions in industrial equipment using machine learning and provides predictive maintenance insights. To act on these insights, organizations can integrate Monitron events with SAP S/4HANA via the SAP BTP. This integration ensures timely actions are taken based on machine learning inferences, enhancing asset reliability and efficiency. The architecture is as follows:

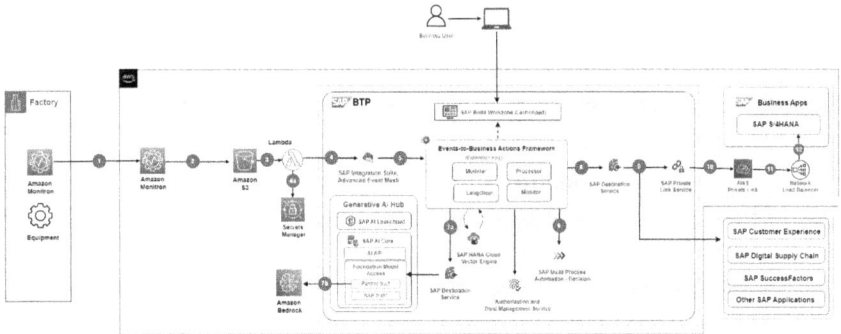

Figure 3.8: Event to business actions framework for AWS Internet of Things

For step-by-step instructions, please visit this link:

https://discovery-center.cloud.sap/missionCatalog/?-search=aws-iot

- **Use case 2**: Auto Stock Replenishment in SAP S/4HANA:

  o SAP S/4HANA can broadcast material movement events through SAP Event Mesh to notify remote applications when stock state changes occur. Utilizing SAP Event Mesh Webhooks and Amazon API Gateway, stock state change notifications can be sent to various event subscribers, enabling auto stock replenishment processes. This integration optimizes inventory management and ensures timely replenishment of stocks:

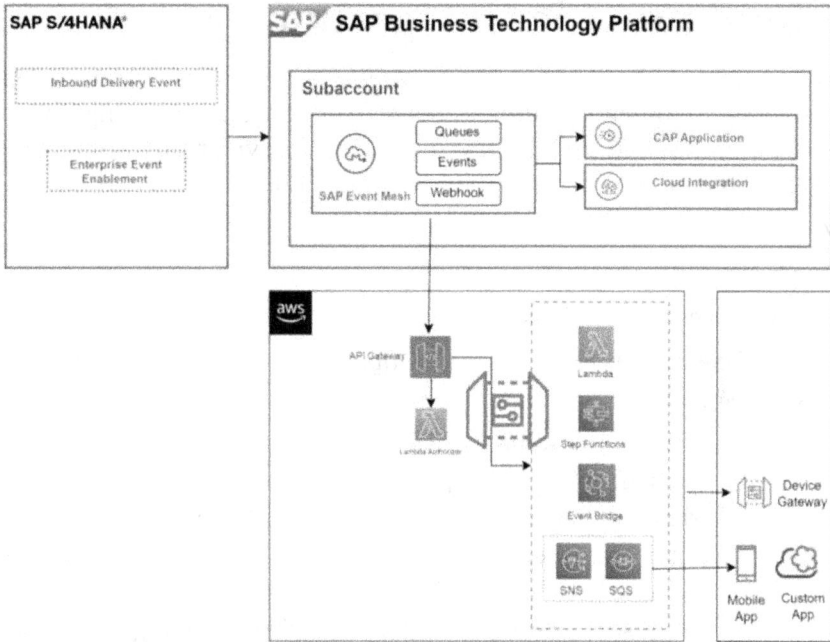

Figure 3.9: Inventory replenishment with SAP BTP and AWS

Machine learning

Machine learning, a subset of **artificial intelligence (AI)**, empowers computers to learn from data and improve their performance over time without being explicitly programmed for each task. Through the analysis of large datasets, machine learning algorithms identify patterns and correlations to make predictions and decisions.

In the realm of **enterprise resource planning (ERP)**, machine learning finds numerous applications:

- **Time series forecasting**: Predicting future trends and demands in supply chain management and sales forecasting.

- **Predictive maintenance and asset optimization**: Utilizing supervised and unsupervised learning to predict equipment failures and optimize asset performance.

- **Computer vision**: Employing image recognition technologies for quality control, process automation, and safety compliance.

Cloud provider integration

Integration with cloud providers like AWS offers unparalleled scalability and computational power for machine learning tasks. Models are trained and deployed on cloud provider platforms, with insights seamlessly integrated into SAP systems.

Use cases

The use cases are as follows:

- **Use case 1:** SAP Integrated Business Planning with Amazon SageMaker:
  - o SAP **Integrated Business Planning** (**IBP**) leverages statistical forecasting and machine learning algorithms for demand sensing. By harnessing scalable cloud provider environments, IBP extends its analytical capabilities beyond SAP S/4HANA to incorporate diverse data sources from social and digital domains. The following is the data federation architecture:

SAP & AWS : IBP and Amazon Forecast/SageMaker

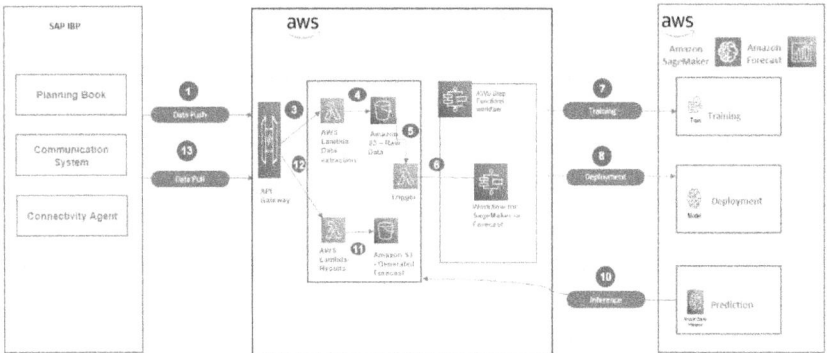

Figure 3.10: SAP IBP External demand sensing with Amazon Sagemaker

- **Use case 2:** Integrate Amazon Rekognition and SAP EHS for PPE Detection:
  - o Safety compliance is crucial in workplaces, requiring the detection of **personal protective equipment** (**PPE**) usage. Integrating Amazon Rekognition with SAP **Environment, Health, and Safety** (**EHS**) automates PPE detection from

camera images, enhancing safety protocols.

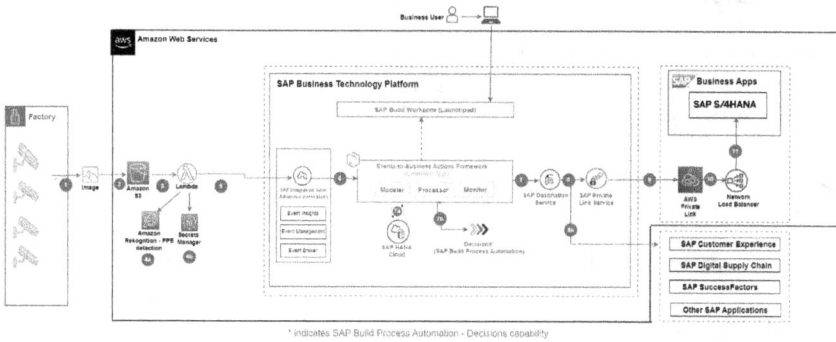

Figure 3.11: *Computer vision-based PPE detection with SAP Advanced event mesh*

For more details, visit SAP Discovery Center Mission:

https://discovery-center.cloud.sap/missiondetail/4352/4635/.

- **Use case 3:** Predict Inventory Allocation with Amazon SageMaker and FedML:

  o Retailers optimize inventory allocation through statistical and machine learning-based forecasting. Data stored in Amazon S3 is federated to SAP Data Warehouse Cloud, facilitating seamless data access for model training. Trained models deployed on Amazon SageMaker or SAP BTP Kyma runtime enable accurate inventory predictions. The following figure depicts the federated data pipelines and architecture:

SAP & AWS : Data-to-Value : Data Federation Architecture for Machine Learning

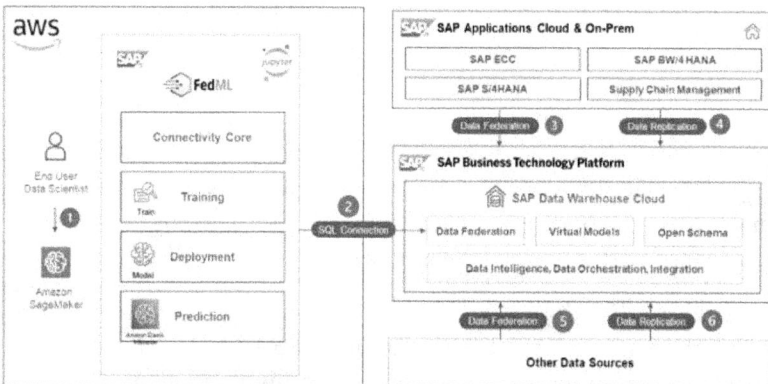

Figure 3.12: *Federated machine learning with Cloud providers*

Explore this use case at SAP Discovery Center Mission: **https://discovery-center.cloud.sap/missiondetail/3656/3699/**.

This chapter underscores the significance of SAP BTP pillars and their integration with cloud providers, offering a comprehensive framework for machine learning adoption and deployment.

Conclusion

The integration of the SAP BTP with cloud providers represents a powerful synergy that drives digital transformation across industries. By leveraging the comprehensive capabilities of SAP BTP alongside the scalability and advanced technologies offered by cloud providers, organizations can unlock new levels of innovation, efficiency, and competitiveness.

This chapter has explored the key components of SAP BTP, the importance of cloud provider integration, and real-world applications across various domains, including data management, application development, and machine learning. We have seen how the combination of SAP's robust enterprise solutions with the flexibility and power of cloud provider platforms enables businesses to adapt quickly to changing market dynamics, harness the full potential of their data, and deliver exceptional customer experiences.

The examples provided throughout this chapter, from integrating Amazon Monitron/AWS IOT services with SAP S/4HANA to leveraging Amazon SageMaker for inventory allocation predictions, demonstrate the practical benefits of this integration. These use cases illustrate how organizations can achieve tangible business outcomes by combining SAP's deep industry expertise with the advanced capabilities of cloud provider platforms.

We have also touched upon SAP's AI Core and Generative AI Hub, highlighting SAP's commitment to providing cutting-edge AI capabilities to its customers. These offerings, which will be explored in greater depth in a later chapter, showcase the potential for AI to transform business processes and decision-making within the SAP ecosystem.

As organizations continue to navigate the complexities of digital transformation, the strategic adoption of SAP BTP and cloud provider integration will be crucial in building resilient, agile, and future-ready enterprise architectures. By embracing these technologies, businesses can position themselves at the forefront of innovation, driving growth and success in an increasingly digital world.

In the next chapter, we look at the crucial topic of designing and building well-architected applications. This upcoming discussion will build upon the foundations laid in this chapter, exploring how organizations can leverage SAP BTP and cloud provider integration to create robust, scalable, and efficient applications that drive business value. We will examine best practices, design patterns, and architectural considerations that ensure applications are not only functional but also optimized for performance, security, and maintainability in the context of SAP BTP and cloud provider environments.

Multiple choice questions

1. **What are the main pillars of SAP Business Technology Platform?**

   a. Development, Testing, Deployment, Maintenance

   b. Apps, Data, Integration, Security

   c. Application Development, Automation, Integration, Data & Analytics, AI

   d. Infrastructure, Platform, Software, Services

2. **Which SAP BTP service is specifically designed for data federation and analytics?**

   a. SAP HANA Cloud

   b. SAP Datasphere

   c. SAP Analytics Cloud

   d. SAP Integration Suite

3. **What is the primary purpose of SAP Integration Suite?**

   a. Database management

   b. Application development

   c. End-to-end integration scenarios

   d. User interface design

4. **In the context of cloud provider integration, what is FedML?**

   a. A federation management language

   b. A library for federated machine learning

c. A federal compliance standard

d. A file encryption system

5. **What role does Amazon SNS play in SAP integration scenarios?**

a. Storage management

b. Network security

c. Notification services

d. System monitoring

6. **What is a key benefit of using the SAP Cloud Application Programming (CAP) model?**

a. Hardware optimization

b. Network configuration

c. Rapid development with built-in services

d. Database administration

7. **Which deployment option is available in SAP BTP for Kubernetes-based applications?**

a. SAP HANA Cloud

b. Kyma runtime

c. Cloud Foundry

d. Neo environment

8. **What is the primary purpose of data mesh architecture?**

a. Centralized data storage

b. Distributed data ownership

c. Data encryption

d. Network optimization

9. **Which AWS service is commonly used for establishing dedicated network connections to SAP systems?**

a. AWS VPC

b. AWS Direct Connect

c. AWS Route 53

d. AWS CloudFront

10. **What is a key feature of SAP Analytics Cloud?**

   a. Database administration

   b. Network monitoring

   c. Augmented analytics and planning

   d. Code compilation

Answers

1. c

   Explanation: SAP BTP is structured around five core pillars: Application Development, Automation, Integration, Data & Analytics, and Artificial Intelligence, each addressing key aspects of modern enterprise technology needs.

2. b

   Explanation: SAP Datasphere (formerly SAP Data Warehouse Cloud) is specifically designed for data federation, providing comprehensive data management and analytics capabilities for aggregating and analyzing data from multiple sources.

3. c

   Explanation: SAP Integration Suite is a comprehensive iPaaS solution that enables organizations to connect applications, processes, and data across landscapes through various integration scenarios, including A2A, B2B, and B2C.

4. b

   Explanation: FedML is a library that enables data scientists to federate data required for machine learning experiments directly on cloud providers' platforms in real-time, supporting machine learning capabilities while maintaining data privacy.

5. c

   Explanation: Amazon SNS provides notification capabilities that can be integrated with SAP applications for sending bulk notifications, enabling efficient communication while reducing costs.

6. c

   Explanation: CAP provides a consistent end-to-end programming model that supports rapid development through out-of-the-box business functionality and best practices, allowing developers to focus on unique features.

7. b

   Explanation: Kyma runtime in SAP BTP provides a Kubernetes-based environment for developing and running microservices and serverless functions, offering flexibility and scalability for cloud-native applications.

8. b

   Explanation: Data mesh architecture decentralizes data management by distributing ownership across various source systems while maintaining standardized interfaces for access and integration.

9. b

   Explanation: AWS Direct Connect provides dedicated network connections between on-premises data centers and AWS infrastructure, enabling secure and reliable connectivity for SAP systems.

10. c

    Explanation: SAP Analytics Cloud combines business intelligence, augmented analytics, and collaborative enterprise planning in a single SaaS solution, enabling data-driven decision-making and planning processes.

Join our book's Discord space

Join the book's Discord Workspace for Latest updates, Offers, Tech happenings around the world, New Release and Sessions with the Authors:

https://discord.bpbonline.com

CHAPTER 4
Introduction to Generative AI

Introduction

Generative AI represents a transformative advancement in artificial intelligence, capable of creating, analyzing, and manipulating content across various modalities. This chapter explores the fundamental concepts of Generative AI and its practical applications within the SAP ecosystem. We examine how organizations can leverage these technologies to enhance business processes, improve decision-making, and create more intelligent enterprise solutions. Through real-world examples and detailed technical discussions, we will demonstrate how SAP's integrated approach to Generative AI, combined with strategic partnerships and robust development tools, enables businesses to harness the full potential of this revolutionary technology. The chapter also explores how manufacturing company XYZ utilizes Generative AI to transform its operations, providing concrete examples of successful implementation and value creation.

Structure

This chapter covers the following topics:

- Understanding Generative AI

- SAP's Business AI approach
- SAP's AI portfolio and offerings
- Generative AI Hub
- Integrating Generative AI into SAP applications
- SAP's AI research and development efforts
- SAP BTP reference architecture for Generative AI
- Real-world examples and use cases
- Amazon Bedrock, Cloud provider integration

Objectives

This chapter provides readers with a comprehensive understanding of Generative AI in the SAP ecosystem and its practical enterprise applications. Readers will gain insights into the core principles of Generative AI and its transformative role in modern enterprise solutions, learning to navigate SAP's AI portfolio and understanding how different offerings create integrated, intelligent solutions.

The chapter equips readers with the knowledge to implement Generative AI solutions using SAP's development tools and frameworks, with emphasis on the Generative AI Hub and best practices for integration with existing SAP systems. A key focus is understanding how Amazon Bedrock integrates with SAP systems and exploring implementation patterns that enable organizations to leverage AWS's foundation models while maintaining SAP's robust security and governance features.

As readers progress through the chapter, they will learn to design scalable Generative AI solutions using SAP BTP, understand cross-platform integration patterns, and recognize various industry-specific use cases. By mastering both SAP's native AI capabilities and their integration with Amazon Bedrock, readers will be prepared to implement sophisticated AI solutions that drive digital transformation while maintaining enterprise standards for security and performance.

Understanding Generative AI

Generative AI is a subset of artificial intelligence that focuses on creating new content, such as text, images, audio, or code, based on learned patterns and rules from existing data. Unlike traditional AI systems designed to recognize or classify existing data, Generative AI aims to generate novel and original content that resembles the training data but is not an exact copy of it.

The key principle behind Generative AI is understanding and learning the underlying structure and patterns in the training data and then using that knowledge to generate new content that adheres to those patterns. This is achieved through various techniques, such as deep learning, neural networks, and probabilistic models.

Key concepts and techniques

To understand how Generative AI works, let us explore some of the key concepts and techniques used in this field:

- **Large Language Models (LLMs):** LLMs are a type of deep learning model that is trained on vast amounts of text data to understand and generate human language. These models, such as **Generative Pre-trained Transformer (GPT)**, can generate coherent and contextually relevant text based on a given prompt or context. LLMs form the foundation for many Generative AI applications, such as natural language generation, language translation, and text summarization.

- **Deep learning**: Deep learning is a subset of machine learning that uses artificial neural networks with multiple layers to learn hierarchical representations of data. In the context of Generative AI, deep learning models, such as **Generative Adversarial Networks (GANs)** and **Variational Autoencoders (VAEs)**, are used to learn the complex patterns and structures in the training data and generate new content.

- **Neural networks**: Neural networks are the building blocks of deep learning models. They consist of interconnected nodes (neurons) organized in layers, where each node performs a simple computation on the input data and passes the result to the next layer. Through training, neural networks learn to adjust the strength of the connections between nodes to minimize the difference between the predicted output and the actual output.

- **Probabilistic models**: Probabilistic models are mathematical frameworks that describe the relationship between variables in terms of probability distributions. In Generative AI, probabilistic models, such as Bayesian Networks and Markov

Chains, are used to capture the underlying structure and dependencies in the training data and generate new samples that follow the same probability distribution.

- **Transfer learning**: Transfer learning is a technique that allows a model trained on one task to be fine-tuned and repurposed for a different but related task. In the context of Generative AI, transfer learning enables the use of pre-trained models, such as language models or image generators, to be adapted for specific domain applications with less training data and faster convergence.

Prompt engineering, RAG, and fine-tuning

To effectively leverage Generative AI models and services, it is important to understand the concepts of prompt engineering, **Retrieval-Augmented Generation** (**RAG**), and fine-tuning. These techniques enable businesses to optimize generative models' performance and output quality for their specific use cases. Let us look at each one of these terminologies.

Prompt engineering

Prompt engineering involves designing and crafting effective prompts or input sequences that guide the generative model to produce the desired output. Effective prompt engineering can significantly improve the quality and coherence of generated content, making it more useful and actionable for business purposes.

The pros are:

- Improves the relevance and accuracy of generated content
- Allows for greater control over the model's output
- Enables users to guide the model towards specific objectives or styles

The cons are:

- Requires iterative experimentation and refinement to find optimal prompts
- It may be time-consuming and require domain expertise
- Prompts may need to be updated as the underlying model or data changes

Here are some examples of good and bad prompts, along with their potential outputs:

- **Good prompts:**
  - **Good prompt:** *Summarize the key points of the following text in 5 bullet points: [text here]*
  - **Good output:**
    - Concise summary of the main ideas
    - Well-structured bullet points
    - Captures the essence of the text without losing important details
    - Maintains the original context and meaning
    - Easy to understand and follow
  - **Good prompt:** *Translate the following sentence from English to French: 'I love exploring new places and trying local cuisines.*
  - **Good output:** J'adore explorer de nouveaux endroits et essayer les cuisines locales.
    - The output accurately translates the sentence while maintaining its meaning and tone.
  - **Good prompt:** *Write a short story about a magical library, focusing on descriptive language and character development. The story should be around 500 words.*
  - **Good output:**
    - A well-crafted short story that includes:
    - Vivid descriptions of the magical library setting
    - Well-developed characters with distinct personalities and motivations
    - A clear plot structure with a beginning, middle, and end
    - Engaging and imaginative storytelling
    - Adheres to the specified word count
- **Bad prompts:**
  - **Bad prompt:** *Tell me about AI.*
  - **Bad output:** The output might be overly broad, lacking focus and structure. It may include irrelevant information

or fail to provide a comprehensive overview of the topic due to the lack of specificity in the prompt.

o **Bad prompt:** *Create a recipe for a delicious meal.*

o **Bad output:** The generated recipe may be incomplete, missing key ingredients or steps. It might also lack coherence and fail to produce a feasible or appetizing meal due to the prompt's absence of guidelines and constraints.

o **Bad prompt:** *Write an article.*

o **Bad output:** The output would likely be extremely generic and unfocused. Without specifying the topic, length, style, or target audience, the generated article may lack purpose, structure, and coherence, making it ineffective and not useful.

Good prompts provide clear instructions, specific details, and constraints guiding AI to generate relevant, coherent, and useful outputs. They often include information about the desired format, length, style, or specific requirements.

Bad prompts, on the other hand, are often vague, open-ended, and lack necessary context or guidelines. They may result in outputs that are irrelevant, inconsistent, or fail to meet the user's expectations due to the lack of direction provided in the prompt.

It is important to craft prompts that are specific, well-defined, and provide sufficient context to ensure that the AI generates accurate, relevant, and high-quality outputs.

Retrieval-Augmented Generation

RAG is a technique that combines information retrieval with generative models to produce more accurate and informative outputs. It enables generative models to access and incorporate relevant information from external knowledge bases or databases during the generation process, allowing the models to generate content grounded in real-world facts and context.

The pros are:

• Incorporates real-world knowledge and facts into generated content

- Improves the accuracy and informative value of the model's output
- Enables the model to handle a wider range of topics and domains

The cons are:

- Requires access to relevant and up-to-date knowledge bases or databases
- This may increase the complexity and latency of the generation process
- The quality of the generated content depends on the quality and coverage of the retrieval sources

Fine-tuning

Fine-tuning involves adapting a pre-trained generative model to a specific domain or task by further training it on a smaller, targeted dataset. Fine-tuning can significantly improve the performance and relevance of generative models for specific use cases, such as generating product descriptions, customer support responses, or industry-specific reports.

The pros are:

- Adapts the model to the specific language, style, and knowledge of a domain
- Improves the performance and relevance of the model for targeted use cases
- Reduces the need for extensive prompt engineering or data preparation

The cons are:

- Requires a sufficient amount of high-quality, domain-specific training data
- It may be computationally expensive and time-consuming, especially for large models
- Overfitting can occur if the fine-tuning dataset is too small or not representative

Embeddings and vector databases in Generative AI

Embeddings and vector databases play a crucial role in enhancing the performance and accuracy of Generative AI models, particularly in the context of RAG and prompt engineering. The details are as follows:

- **Embeddings:**
  - Embeddings are dense vector representations of data points, such as words, sentences, or documents, in a high-dimensional space. In the context of Generative AI, embeddings are used to represent the semantic meaning and relationships between different pieces of information.
  - By converting textual data into embeddings, Generative AI models can better understand and process the information, enabling more accurate and contextually relevant outputs. Embeddings capture the semantic similarity between data points, allowing the model to identify related concepts and perform tasks like semantic search, clustering, and information retrieval.
  - Common embedding techniques used in Generative AI include word embeddings (e.g., Word2Vec, GloVe), sentence embeddings (e.g., BERT, RoBERTa), and document embeddings (e.g., Doc2Vec). These embeddings are typically pre-trained on large corpora of text data and can be fine-tuned for specific domains or tasks.

- **Vector databases:**
  - Vector databases, or embedding databases, are specialized storage systems designed to store efficiently, index, and retrieve embeddings. Unlike traditional databases that store structured data, vector databases are optimized for handling high-dimensional vectors.
  - In Generative AI, vector databases are a knowledge repository for storing embeddings of various data sources, such as documents, articles, or knowledge bases. By organizing the embeddings in a vector database, Generative AI models can quickly retrieve relevant information based on semantic similarity.

o Vector databases offer several advantages for Generative AI:

- **Efficient similarity search**: Vector databases use **approximate nearest neighbor (ANN)** algorithms to quickly find the most similar embeddings to a given query embedding, enabling fast information retrieval.

- **Scalability**: Vector databases can handle large-scale datasets and support efficient indexing and retrieval of millions or even billions of embeddings.

- **Semantic understanding**: By storing embeddings, vector databases enable Generative AI models to capture the semantic relationships between data points, facilitating better understanding and generation of contextually relevant outputs.

o Popular vector database solutions used in Generative AI include Faiss, Annoy, Hnswlib, and Milvus.

- **Retrieval Augmented Generation:**

o RAG is a technique that combines information retrieval with Generative AI models to improve the accuracy and relevance of generated outputs. RAG leverages embeddings and vector databases to retrieve relevant information from external knowledge sources and incorporate it into the generation process.

o In RAG, the Generative AI model is augmented with a retrieval component that searches the vector database for the most relevant embeddings based on the input query or prompt. The retrieved information is then fed into the generative model along with the original prompt, providing additional context and knowledge to guide the generation process.

o By incorporating retrieved information, RAG enables Generative AI models to produce more accurate, informative, and contextually relevant outputs. It helps mitigate the limitations of relying solely on the model's pre-trained knowledge and allows for the integration of up-to-date and domain-specific information. The following figure illustrates the architecture for RAG with the Knowledge repository and LLMs:

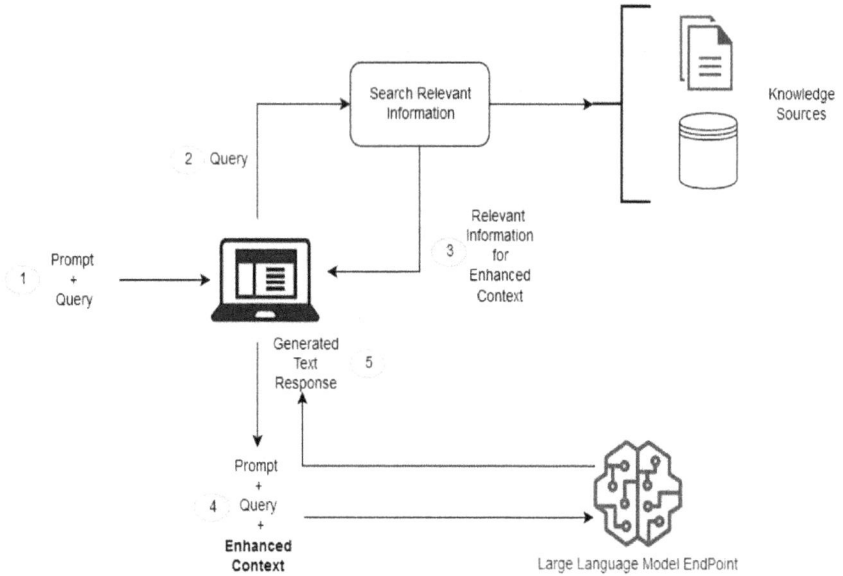

Figure 4.1: *Retrieval Augmented Generation with Large Language Models*

- **Prompt engineering with embeddings:**
  - Prompt engineering is the process of designing effective prompts to guide Generative AI models toward desired outputs. Embeddings can be leveraged in prompt engineering to provide additional context and improve the quality of generated responses.

  - One approach is to use embeddings to retrieve relevant information from a vector database and include it in the prompt. By incorporating retrieved knowledge into the prompt, the Generative AI model can better understand the context and generate more accurate and informative responses.

  - Another technique is to use embeddings to create semantic prompts. Instead of using raw text as prompts, semantic prompts combine relevant embeddings that capture the desired semantic meaning. This allows for more precise and targeted prompting, improving output quality.

○ Prompt engineering with embeddings requires careful consideration of factors such as the quality and relevance of the retrieved information, the appropriate embedding techniques to use, and the design of effective prompts that leverage the retrieved knowledge.

As Generative AI continues to evolve, integrating embeddings and vector databases will play a crucial role in enabling more sophisticated and knowledge-intensive applications. By leveraging these techniques, developers and researchers can build Generative AI models that effectively combine pre-trained knowledge with external information sources, unlocking new possibilities for natural language generation, question answering, and content creation.

Applications and use cases

Generative AI has various applications and use cases across various industries and domains. Let us consider how our example manufacturing company, XYZ, is leveraging Generative AI to transform its operations:

- **Customer communication**: XYZ is using Generative AI to enhance its customer communication through SAP **Customer for Commerce (C4C)**. By integrating Generative AI capabilities into its C4C system, XYZ can automatically generate personalized email responses, chat messages, and product recommendations based on customer inquiries and preferences. This not only improves customer service efficiency but also provides a more engaging and tailored experience for the customers.

- **Knowledge base creation**: XYZ is utilizing Generative AI to create a comprehensive knowledge base for its SAP end-users. By training a Generative AI model on existing documentation, user manuals, and support tickets, XYZ can automatically generate content for frequently asked questions, troubleshooting guides, and step-by-step tutorials. This knowledge base is then made accessible through a chatbot, allowing users to quickly find answers to their queries, such as, *How to create a return sales order for the core returns process?* without needing to manually search through extensive documentation.

- **Recipe generation**: As a manufacturing company, XYZ is always looking for ways to innovate its products and formulations. By leveraging Generative AI, XYZ can explore new recipe ideas for its existing products by training a model on its current product catalog, ingredient lists, and manufacturing processes. The Generative AI model can then suggest novel combinations of ingredients, proportions, and processing parameters that have a high likelihood of resulting in viable and interesting product variations. This enables XYZ to accelerate its product development cycles and stay ahead of the competition.

- **Code completion**: XYZ's software development team is using Generative AI to assist in code completion and generation. By training a Generative AI model on the company's existing codebase and programming patterns, developers can receive intelligent suggestions and auto-completions as they write code. This not only speeds up the development process but also promotes consistency and adherence to best practices across the team.

- **Synthetic data generation**: In situations where real-world data is scarce, expensive, or difficult to obtain, XYZ is using Generative AI to create synthetic datasets that mimic the characteristics and distributions of the real data. These synthetic datasets can be used to train and validate machine learning models, test software systems, or simulate various scenarios without the need for actual data. This is particularly useful in domains such as quality control, where generating realistic defect images can help improve the accuracy of visual inspection systems.

- **Demand forecasting**: In the supply chain context, accurate demand forecasting is crucial for optimizing inventory levels, reducing waste, and improving customer satisfaction. XYZ is using Generative AI to enhance its demand forecasting capabilities by training models on historical sales data, market trends, and external factors such as weather and economic indicators. The Generative AI model can then simulate future demand scenarios, considering the complex interdependencies and uncertainties in the supply chain. This enables XYZ to make more informed decisions around production planning, resource allocation, and inventory management.

- **Predictive maintenance:** Industrial equipment and machinery are subject to wear and tear over time, leading to unplanned downtime and costly repairs. XYZ is leveraging Generative AI to predict when equipment is likely to fail and schedule proactive maintenance activities. By training a Generative AI model on sensor data, maintenance logs, and failure histories, the system can generate realistic failure scenarios and estimate the remaining useful life of equipment. This allows XYZ to optimize its maintenance strategies, reduce downtime, and extend the lifespan of its assets.

- **Generative design:** In the product design and engineering space, Generative AI is being used to explore novel design solutions that optimize for specific criteria such as performance, cost, and manufacturability. XYZ is applying Generative AI to its design processes by specifying the design goals, constraints, and materials and letting the AI generate a range of design alternatives that meet those requirements. The generated designs can then be evaluated and refined by human engineers, leading to faster iteration cycles and more innovative solutions.

- **Anomaly detection:** In industrial settings, detecting anomalies and deviations from normal operating conditions is essential for ensuring product quality, safety, and efficiency. XYZ is using Generative AI to learn its production processes' normal patterns and behaviors and identify any anomalies or outliers in real-time. By training a Generative AI model on sensor data, log files, and quality metrics, the system can generate a baseline of normal operation and flag any deviations that may indicate potential issues such as equipment malfunction, process drift, or quality defects.

- **Supply chain optimization:** Generative AI can also be applied to optimize various aspects of the supply chain, from logistics and transportation to warehouse management and inventory allocation. XYZ is using Generative AI to simulate and optimize its supply chain network by generating scenarios that consider factors such as demand variability, lead times, transportation costs, and capacity constraints. The AI can then recommend optimal network configurations, inventory policies, and transportation routes that minimize costs and maximize service levels.

These additional examples demonstrate how Generative AI transforms the industrial and supply chain landscape, enabling companies like XYZ to drive efficiency, innovation, and competitive advantage. By leveraging the power of Generative AI across various functions and processes, organizations can unlock new insights, automate complex tasks, and make better decisions in the face of uncertainty and change.

As we move forward in this book, we will explore in more detail how SAP's Generative AI offerings, such as SAP Joule and SAP AI Business Services, empower customers to implement these use cases and realize the benefits of Generative AI in their specific industry contexts.

SAP's Business AI approach

SAP's approach to Business AI combines enterprise expertise with cutting-edge AI capabilities to deliver practical, scalable solutions for business transformation. This comprehensive framework ensures that AI implementations are relevant, reliable, and responsible while delivering measurable business value. The Salient aspects of this approach will be discussed in the following section.

AI capabilities driving business value

SAP's Business AI approach focuses on three main areas where AI is applied to drive business value: automation, natural user experience, insights, optimization, and predictions. AI and machine learning algorithms are used to automate repetitive tasks, allowing employees to focus on more complex business problems, innovation, and customer engagement. Generative AI, in particular, facilitates more human-like interaction with machines, enabling users to interact with SAP systems using natural language, even for tasks that are not performed daily. AI also provides insights, optimization, and predictions by analyzing vast amounts of data, helping users make data-driven decisions and receive proactive recommendations.

The following figure illustrates SAP's comprehensive approach to AI-driven business value creation, showing the interrelationship between automation, user experience, and intelligent insights:

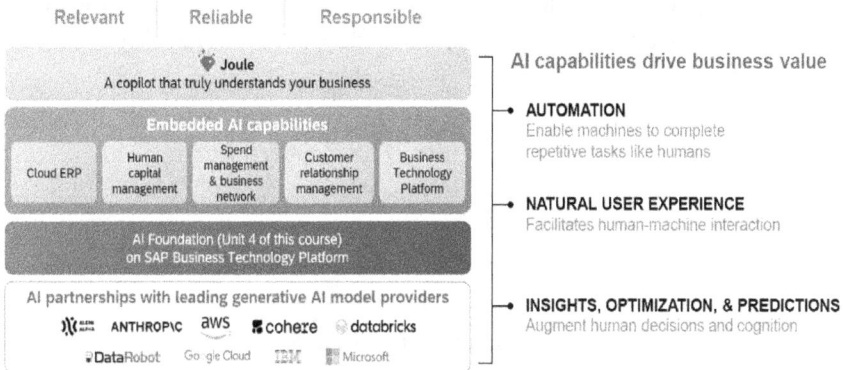

Figure 4.2: *SAP Business AI value creation framework*

Relevance, reliability, and responsibility in AI applications

SAP ensures that AI applications are relevant to the business context and processes, reliable by using the right data and integration methods, and responsible by adhering to ethical guidelines and data compliance regulations. SAP's AI applications are deeply embedded into its solutions, ensuring that the right data is used and that users can see where AI is applied and how recommendations are generated. SAP has a robust ethical framework and processes to avoid bias and ensure data privacy compliance, such as GDPR.

SAP's AI ecosystem partnerships and investments

SAP has formed partnerships with leading Generative AI model providers to leverage the latest advancements in LLMs and Generative AI algorithms across various business contexts. These partnerships complement SAP's internal development of deep learning models, HANA database-specific algorithms, and the evolution towards SAP-optimized foundation models as part of its AI foundation stack.

SAP's AI portfolio and offerings

SAP's comprehensive AI portfolio follows a layered architecture that combines foundational technologies, development tools, and enterprise-ready solutions. This integrated suite is structured in three distinct layers, each serving specific needs while maintaining seamless integration across the stack:

- **Large Language Models:** At the foundation are the LLMs that power SAP's AI capabilities. This layer comprises:
  o SAP-developed specialized models for enterprise contexts
  o Partner ecosystem contributions include:
    ▪ Microsoft Azure OpenAI models
    ▪ Anthropic's Claude models via Amazon Bedrock
    ▪ Other leading AI providers
  o Integration frameworks for incorporating new foundation models

- **AI Foundation in SAP BTP:** The AI Foundation layer within SAP Business Technology Platform provides developers with tools and services to build AI-enabled applications:
  o SAP AI Core for model deployment and management
  o SAP AI Launchpad for centralized AI application oversight
  o Generative AI Hub for development and integration
  o Vector database capabilities in SAP HANA
  o APIs and SDKs for AI service consumption
  o Development tools and frameworks

- **Embedded AI and copilot:** At the top of the stack are pre-built AI capabilities and intelligent interfaces:
  o Embedded AI features within SAP's SaaS applications:
    ▪ Intelligent candidate matching in SAP SuccessFactors
    ▪ Smart spend analysis in SAP Concur
    ▪ Automated invoice processing in SAP Ariba
    ▪ Predictive analytics in SAP S/4HANA
  o **SAP Joule**: A conversational AI copilot that:
    ▪ Provides natural language interaction across SAP applications
    ▪ Enables context-aware assistance and recommendations
    ▪ Automates complex workflows through conversation

- Integrates with existing business processes

- Offers personalized insights and suggestions

This layered architecture ensures that organizations can leverage AI capabilities at multiple levels, from building custom AI applications using foundation models to utilizing pre-built AI features in SAP solutions, all unified through the conversational interface of SAP Joule.

The following figure illustrates SAP's three-layer AI portfolio architecture, showing the progression from foundation models to end-user applications:

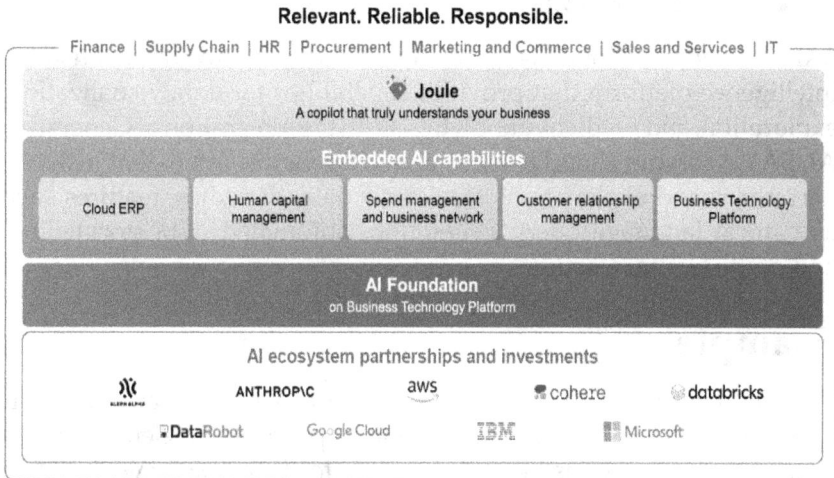

Figure 4.3: SAP AI portfolio architecture

Let us study the BTP services comprising the AI foundation layer.

SAP AI Core

SAP AI Core is a set of AI services and tools that enable businesses to build, deploy, and manage AI applications across various domains. While SAP does not have its own LLM, SAP AI Core provides a framework for integrating and leveraging third-party LLMs and AI models, allowing customers to benefit from the latest advancements in Generative AI while seamlessly integrating them into their SAP applications and processes.

SAP Datasphere

SAP Datasphere is a comprehensive data management and integration platform that enables businesses to harness the full potential of their data assets across multiple cloud environments. It provides capabilities for data cataloging, integration, quality, and governance. In the context of Generative AI, SAP Datasphere enables the aggregation and preparation of large and diverse datasets that can be used to train generative models.

SAP Analytics Cloud

SAP Analytics Cloud is a cloud-based analytics and business intelligence platform that provides capabilities for data visualization, exploration, and predictive analytics. With the integration of Generative AI, SAP Analytics Cloud enables users to generate intelligent insights, narratives, and explanations from their data, including features such as natural language query generation, automated data storytelling, and predictive forecasting.

Example

Fictional company XYZ uses SAP Analytics Cloud to analyze their sales data. With the *Ask a Question* feature powered by Generative AI, users can ask questions like *What was the total revenue for product X in Q1?* in natural language. SAP Analytics Cloud generates a response and visualizes the relevant data, enabling users to quickly gain insights without the need for complex queries or manual data exploration.

SAP AI Business Services

SAP AI Business Services are a suite of pre-trained AI models and services that can be easily integrated into SAP applications and business processes. These services cover various domains, such as document processing, invoice management, and Intelligent Robotic Process Automation. Generative AI capabilities are embedded into these services, enabling tasks such as generating purchase order descriptions or creating synthetic training data for invoice matching.

SAP HANA Vector DB

SAP HANA Vector DB for Generative AI SAP HANA Vector DB is a vector database that enables efficient storage and retrieval of vector embeddings, which are essential for grounding Generative AI models. By storing embeddings of enterprise data, such as product information, customer profiles, and knowledge articles, SAP HANA Vector DB allows Generative AI models to access contextually relevant information during inference.

Generative AI Hub

The Generative AI Hub represents SAP's centralized platform for developing, deploying, and managing Generative AI applications. It provides a comprehensive suite of tools and services that enable organizations to leverage the latest advances in AI while maintaining enterprise-grade security and governance. The following architecture shows the key components and interactions within the Generative AI Hub, highlighting its role in the broader SAP ecosystem:

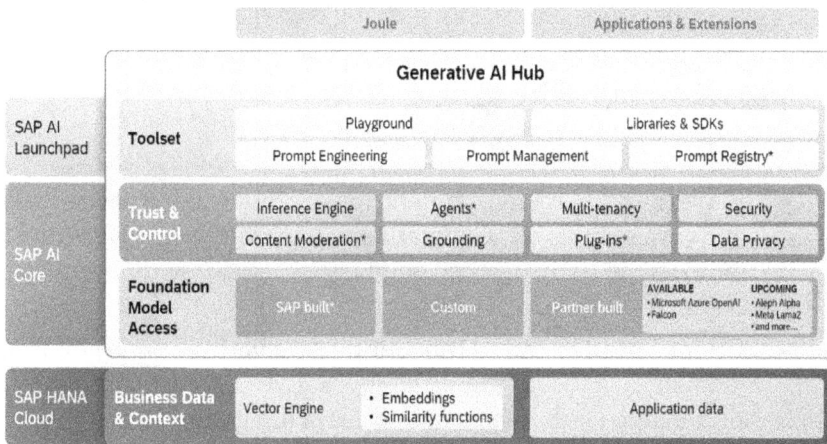

Figure 4.4: Generative AI Hub in AI foundation

Access to foundation models via SAP AI Core

The Generative AI Hub provides developers instant access to partner-built foundation models, such as Microsoft Azure OpenAI models (e.g., GPT-3) and Anthropic's Constitutional AI models (e.g., Claude).

In the future, SAP plans to add more foundation models from partners like Aleph Alpha and Meta. This allows developers to integrate and experiment with various foundation models in their applications.

Toolset for Generative AI development

The Generative AI Hub offers tools and services to streamline the development of Generative AI applications. These include the following:

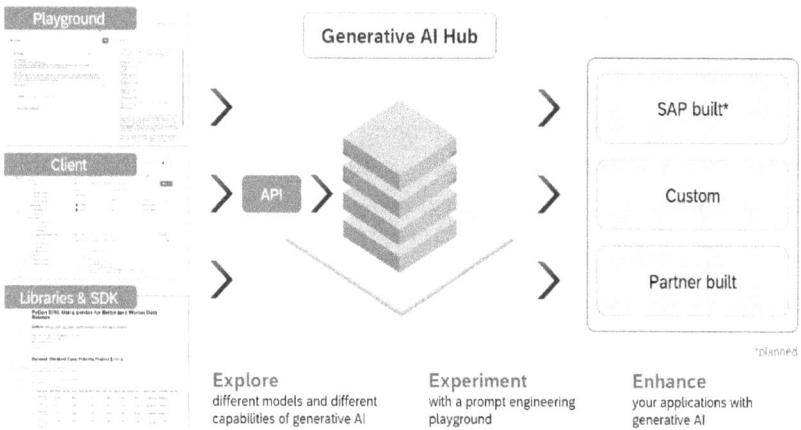

Figure 4.5: SAP Generative AI hub

- **Playground**: An environment for exploring different models and capabilities of Generative AI, enabling developers to experiment with prompt engineering and test different use cases.

- **Client libraries and SDKs**: Supporting various programming languages and runtimes, such as Python, to facilitate the productive use of the Generative AI Hub in applications.

- **Prompt management**: Tools for managing and versioning prompts, allowing developers to optimize and refine their prompts over time.

For detailed examples, please visit https://discovery-center.cloud.sap/missions/?appType=platform&category=all&type=platform&search=generative-ai.

Trust and control in Generative AI applications

The Generative AI Hub provides features to ensure trust and control in Generative AI applications, such as:

- **Security and data privacy**: Ensuring that applications are natively integrated with SAP security and comply with data privacy regulations.

- **Model response grounding**: Controlling the model's output by providing context from enterprise data, reducing the risk of hallucinations, and generating more relevant responses.

- **Multi-tenancy support**: Enabling the development of multi-tenant applications that can serve multiple customers while maintaining data isolation and security.

Integrating Generative AI into SAP applications

SAP offers multiple approaches for integrating Generative AI capabilities into existing applications and business processes. Here are some salient integration patterns and technologies that organizations can leverage to enhance their SAP landscape with AI capabilities:

- **Document Information Extraction**: SAP's **Document Information Extraction (DIE)** service uses Generative AI to automatically extract entities and relevant information from various business documents, such as invoices, purchase orders, and contracts. The premium version of DIE, powered by LLMs, supports a wide range of document types and languages out of the box, enabling businesses to automate document processing at scale.

  o **Example:** In the fictional company XYZ, the accounts payable department receives a large volume of invoices from suppliers in different formats and languages. By integrating SAP's DIE service into their invoice processing workflow, XYZ can automatically extract key information such as invoice numbers, supplier names, and line items, reducing manual data entry and accelerating the invoice approval process.

- **Intelligent Robotic Process Automation:** SAP's **Intelligent Robotic Process Automation (RPA)** solution leverages Generative AI to automate repetitive and rule-based tasks, such as data entry, data validation, and report generation. By training generative models on user actions and business processes, intelligent bots can mimic human behavior and adapt to changing requirements, enabling businesses to scale their automation efforts.

- **Natural language interaction with SAP systems:** Generative AI enables users to interact with SAP systems using natural language, making it easier to access information, perform tasks, and navigate complex processes. Examples include:

  o **SAP Analytics Cloud**: The *Ask a Question* feature allows users to ask questions about their data in natural language and receive instant insights and visualizations.

  o **SAP Joule**: A digital assistant that guides users through various tasks and processes across SAP applications, providing contextual support and generating content based on user input.

Roadmap

In the fictional company XYZ, a manager wants to create a job posting for a new position. Using SAP Joule, the manager can simply ask, *Create a job posting for a store manager in Geneva*. Joule guides the manager through the process, auto-filling relevant information from existing employee profiles, generating a job description based on the provided context, and initiating the necessary approval workflows in SAP SuccessFactors.

There are plenty of tutorials available in the SAP community: **https://discovery-center.cloud.sap/missions/?appType=platform&category ry=all&type=platform&search=generative-ai** and it is constantly getting updated.

SAP Joule represents SAP's strategic investment in AI-powered assistance across its application suite. As SAP's copilot, Joule aims to transform how users interact with SAP systems through natural language processing and contextual understanding.

Strategic roadmap

SAP has announced an ambitious expansion plan for Joule's capabilities through 2025. Here is the planned rollout:

- **Q4 2024 planned features**
  - **Mobile integration**
    - Integration with SAP Mobile Start
    - Mobile approval workflows
    - On-the-go feedback capabilities
    - Real-time mobile assistance
- **Q4 2024 planned integrations**
  - SAP Mobile Start
  - SAP Concur solutions (beta)
  - SAP Sales Cloud
  - SAP LeanIX solutions
  - SAP Signavio solutions
- **Q1 2025 planned features**
  - **Enhanced developer support**
    - ABAP code generation
    - Automated unit test creation
    - Code explanation capabilities
    - Development productivity tools
  - **Supply chain intelligence**
    - What-if scenario analysis
    - Up to 50% faster planning workflows
    - Root cause analysis for delays
    - Automated corrective action suggestions
  - **Advanced analytics**
    - Natural language data queries
    - Enhanced insight generation
    - Cross-application data analysis
    - Simplified reporting workflows

- **Q1 2025 planned integrations**
  - o   SAP Ariba solutions
  - o   SAP Concur solutions (General Availability)
  - o   SAP Business Network
  - o   SAP Service Cloud
  - o   SAP Fieldglass solutions
- **Implementation considerations:** Organizations planning to leverage Joule should:
  - o   Assess their readiness for AI-powered assistance
  - o   Plan for phased adoption aligned with the release schedule
  - o   Consider integration requirements with existing systems
  - o   Prepare training programs for users
  - o   Monitor SAP's roadmap for updates and changes

Note: All future dates and capabilities are based on SAP's published plans and are subject to change. Organizations should consult SAP's official documentation and roadmap for the most current information.

SAP's AI research and development efforts

SAP's approach to AI research and development combines academic partnerships, internal innovation, and practical business applications. This comprehensive strategy ensures that theoretical advances can be quickly transformed into enterprise-ready solutions. Some areas of research include:

- **Multimodal generation:** SAP is exploring advanced techniques for generating content that spans multiple modalities, such as text, images, and speech. This includes research into cross-modal transfer learning, where knowledge learned in one modality can be transferred and applied to another.
- **Controllable generation:** SAP is investigating methods for controlling and guiding the output of generative models based on specific attributes, styles, or constraints, such as conditional generation, style transfer, and attribute manipulation. This enables businesses to generate content that aligns with

their brand guidelines, tone of voice, and target audience preferences.

- **Efficient training and inference:** SAP is researching ways to make the training and inference of generative models more efficient and scalable, using techniques like model compression, quantization, and distributed training. This enables the deployment of generative models on resource-constrained devices and real-time applications.

- **Explainable and trustworthy AI:** SAP is committed to developing Generative AI solutions that are transparent, interpretable, and trustworthy. This includes research into methods for explaining the decisions and outputs of generative models, detecting and mitigating biases, and ensuring the ethical and responsible use of Generative AI.

SAP BTP reference architecture for Generative AI

The SAP BTP reference architecture for Generative AI provides a blueprint for building scalable and secure Generative AI applications on the SAP **Business Technology Platform** (**BTP**). The architecture showcases how various components, such as the Generative AI Hub, SAP AI Core, CAP Application, and SAP HANA Cloud, can be integrated to create end-to-end Generative AI solutions. The following figure illustrates the complete reference architecture, showing how different components interact to enable end-to-end Generative AI solutions:

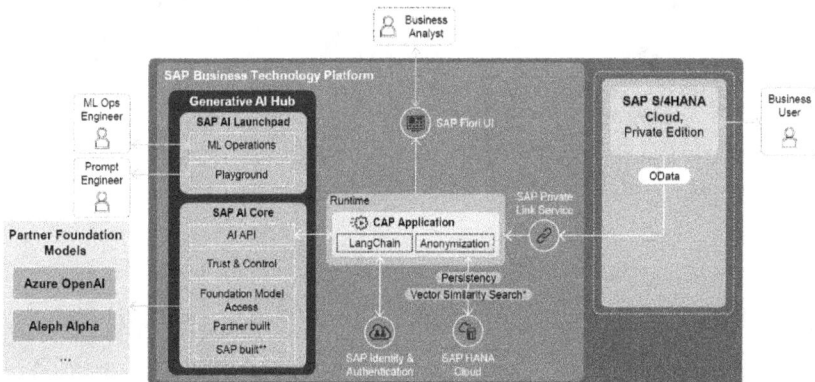

Figure 4.6: SAP CAP application with Generative AI

Key components and their roles

The key components of the SAP BTP reference architecture for Generative AI include:

- **Generative AI Hub**: Provides access to foundation models, tools for prompt engineering, and trust and control features.
- **SAP AI Core**: Enables the development, deployment, and management of AI applications, including Generative AI.
- **SAP HANA Cloud**: Serves as the data foundation for Generative AI applications, providing capabilities for data storage, processing, and analytics.
- **SAP Fiori UI**: Provides a user-friendly interface for interacting with Generative AI applications.
- **SAP Private Link Service**: Ensures secure connectivity between components and external systems.
- Full stack CAP application that integrates with SAP S/4 HANA via RFC or odata protocols.

Integration with SAP systems and AI models

The reference architecture below demonstrates how Generative AI applications can be integrated with various SAP systems and applications, such as SAP S/4HANA and SAP SuccessFactors. This integration allows businesses to leverage Generative AI capabilities within their existing SAP landscapes, enabling intelligent automation, enhanced decision-making, and improved user experiences.

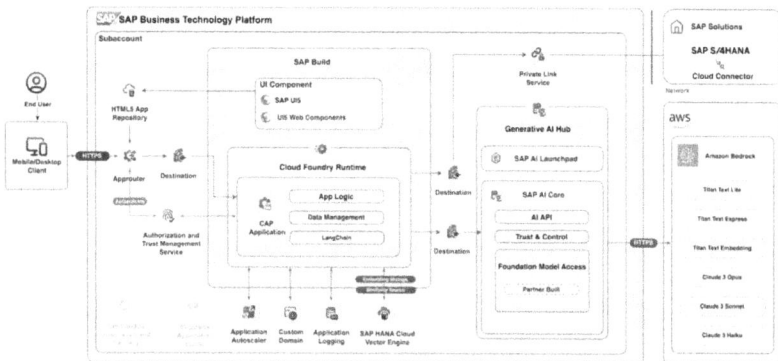

Figure 4.7: Generative AI reference architecture

This architecture diagram illustrates the end-to-end flow of a Generative AI-enabled application in the SAP ecosystem, consisting of several key components:

- **Client layer:**
  - Starts with an End User accessing the system through a Mobile/Desktop Client
  - Connects via HTTPS to the application
  - Uses HTML5 App Repository for web content storage
- **Security layer:**
  - Implements Authentication and Trust Management Service
  - Includes Approuter for handling routing and authentication
  - Provides Destination service for connection management
- **Application layer (SAP Build):** The two main components are:
  - **UI component:**
    - SAP UI5 components
    - UI5 Web Components
  - **Cloud Foundry runtime:** CAP Application containing:
    - App Logic
    - Data Management
    - LaunchPad integration
- **Integration services:**
  - Application autoscaler for scaling
  - Custom domain management
  - Application logging
  - SAP HANA Cloud Vector Engine for vector storage
- **AI services layer:**
  - Generative AI Hub providing central access
  - SAP AI Launchpad for management
  - SAP AI Core contains:
    - AI API
    - Trust and control mechanisms

- Foundation model access
- Partner built models
- **External integration:**
  o Private Link Service for secure connectivity
  o Connection to SAP S/4HANA via Cloud Connector
  o Integration with Amazon Bedrock services:
    - Titan Text Lite
    - Titan Text Express
    - Titan Text Embedding
    - Claude 3 Opus
    - Claude 3 Sonnet
    - Claude Haiku
- **Supporting components:**
  o Continuous Integration and Delivery
  o Business Application Studio for development
  o Full monitoring and logging capabilities

This architecture ensures secure, scalable, and efficient integration of Generative AI capabilities within the SAP ecosystem while maintaining enterprise-grade security and performance standards.

Real-world examples and use cases

Some real-world examples and use cases are as follows:

- **Enhancing customer support with email insights and automation:** The transcript provides an example of a fictional company using Generative AI to enhance their customer support processes. By analyzing incoming emails using LLMs, the company can automatically categorize issues, detect sentiment, and assess urgency. The system can also generate potential responses based on historical data and context, improving response times and quality.
- **Generating contextual responses with SAP Joule:** SAP Joule, a digital assistant powered by Generative AI, can help users navigate various tasks and processes across SAP applications. In the example provided, a manager uses SAP

Joule to create a job posting in SAP SuccessFactors. SAP Joule guides the manager through the process, auto filling relevant information, generating a job description, and initiating approval workflows, demonstrating how Generative AI can streamline complex tasks and improve productivity.

- **Improving decision-making with natural language querying in SAP Analytics Cloud:** SAP Analytics Cloud integrates Generative AI capabilities to enable users to ask questions about their data in natural language. In the demo, a user asks, *Which product has the lowest cost and the lowest sales cost?* SAP Analytics Cloud processes the query, generates visualizations, and applies the necessary filters and sorting to provide the requested insights. This showcases how Generative AI can democratize data analysis and help users make data-driven decisions more easily.

Amazon Bedrock, Cloud provider integration

Amazon Bedrock is a fully managed AI service provided by **Amazon Web Services (AWS)** that enables developers and businesses to build, train, and easily deploy LLMs and Generative AI applications. It offers a comprehensive suite of tools and features to streamline the development process and make Generative AI more accessible and scalable:

- **Foundation models:** Amazon Bedrock provides access to a wide range of pre-trained foundation models, including models developed by leading AI research organizations such as Anthropic, AI21 Labs, and Cohere. These models cover various domains and tasks, including natural language processing, question answering, text generation, and more.

  By leveraging these foundation models, developers can quickly build powerful Generative AI applications without the need for extensive training data or computational resources. Amazon Bedrock takes care of hosting, scaling, and updating the models, allowing developers to focus on creating value-added applications.

- **Fine-tuning and customization:** Amazon Bedrock offers tools and workflows for fine-tuning foundation models to adapt them to specific domains or tasks. Developers can upload their own training data and use Bedrock's fine-tuning capabilities to create custom models that are tailored to their specific use cases.

Fine-tuning allows developers to improve the performance and accuracy of the foundation models by incorporating domain-specific knowledge and terminology. This enables the creation of highly specialized Generative AI applications that can understand and generate content in a particular context.

- **Prompt engineering:** Amazon Bedrock provides a user-friendly interface for prompt engineering, which is the process of designing effective prompts to guide the Generative AI models toward desired outputs. Developers can use Bedrock's prompt engineering tools to create, test, and refine prompts that elicit accurate and relevant responses from the models.

Bedrock offers a prompt library with predefined templates and examples for common use cases, making it easier for developers to get started with prompt engineering. It also supports the creation of custom prompts and the ability to incorporate retrieved information from external sources to enhance the prompts.

- **Integration with AWS Services:** Amazon Bedrock seamlessly integrates with other AWS services, enabling developers to build end-to-end Generative AI workflows. It can be used in conjunction with services like Amazon S3 for data storage, Amazon SageMaker for model training and deployment, and AWS Lambda for serverless computing.

This integration allows developers to leverage the full capabilities of the AWS ecosystem to build scalable and efficient Generative AI applications. They can easily incorporate data from various sources, automate model training and deployment pipelines, and deploy their applications in a highly available and fault-tolerant manner.

- **Security and compliance:** Amazon Bedrock prioritizes security and compliance, ensuring that Generative AI applications built on the platform adhere to the highest standards of data protection and privacy. It provides encryption for data at rest and in transit, secure access control mechanisms, and compliance with various industry regulations.

Bedrock integrates with AWS **Identity and Access Management (IAM)** to enable fine-grained access control and authorization. Developers can define IAM policies to specify permissions and access levels for different users and roles, ensuring that only authorized individuals can access and interact with the Generative AI resources.

Additionally, Amazon Bedrock leverages AWS **Key Management Service (KMS)** for secure key management and encryption. It allows developers to use customer-managed keys or AWS-managed keys to encrypt sensitive data, such as training datasets and model artifacts, adding an extra layer of security.

Bedrock also offers tools for content filtering and moderation, helping developers prevent the generation of inappropriate or harmful content. It provides flexibility to configure content filters based on specific requirements and supports automated content moderation workflows.

- **Cost optimization:** Amazon Bedrock provides various cost optimization features and best practices to help developers and businesses manage and optimize their spending on Generative AI applications. It offers a pay-as-you-go pricing model, allowing users to pay only for the resources they consume without any upfront costs or long-term commitments.

  Bedrock provides cost monitoring and budgeting tools to give users visibility into their resource usage and costs. Developers can set up cost alerts and notifications to stay informed about their spending and avoid unexpected charges. They can also define budget thresholds and receive alerts when their usage exceeds predefined limits.

  Moreover, Amazon Bedrock offers cost-saving options such as spot instances and reserved instances. Spot instances allow users to bid on spare compute capacity at a significantly lower price compared to on-demand instances. Reserved instances enable users to commit to a specific instance type and duration in exchange for a discounted rate.

  Bedrock also provides recommendations and best practices for cost optimization, such as right-sizing instances, using efficient data storage options, and leveraging auto-scaling to automatically adjust resources based on demand. By following these best practices and utilizing the cost optimization features, developers can ensure that their Generative AI applications are running cost-effectively.

- **Scalability and performance:** Amazon Bedrock is designed to handle the scalability and performance demands of Generative AI applications. It automatically scales the underlying infrastructure based on the workload, ensuring optimal performance and efficient resource utilization.

  Bedrock's distributed architecture allows for the processing of large volumes of data and the handling of high-concurrency requests. It leverages advanced techniques like model parallelism and data parallelism to optimize the performance of foundation models and enable faster generation of outputs.

- **Monitoring and logging:** Amazon Bedrock provides comprehensive monitoring and logging capabilities to help developers track the performance and usage of their Generative AI applications. It integrates with Amazon CloudWatch, enabling real-time monitoring of metrics, logs, and events.

  Developers can set up alerts and notifications based on predefined thresholds, allowing them to proactively identify and address any issues or anomalies. Bedrock also generates detailed logs and audit trails, facilitating debugging, troubleshooting, and compliance auditing.

Furthermore, Amazon Bedrock offers cost optimization features and best practices to help developers and businesses manage their spending on Generative AI applications. With pay-as-you-go pricing, cost-monitoring tools, and cost-saving options, Bedrock enables users to run their applications cost-effectively while still achieving their desired performance and scalability.

SAP customers can use Amazon Bedrock and integrate SAP ODATA and RFC protocols or real-time scenarios like summarizing results or document comprehension.

The following is a reference architecture for Amazon IOT integration with SAP Plant maintenance. Here, Gen AI is used to summarize IOT signal information into simple English and meaningful actions:

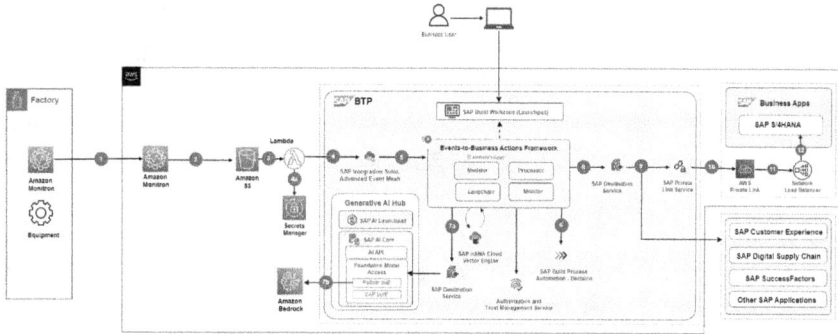

Figure 4.8: AWS IoT integration with SAP Asset management using Generative AI

This is available as a mission in SAP Discovery Center: **https://discovery-center.cloud.sap/missiondetail/4345/4628/**.

The key features of Amazon Bedrock are as follows:

- **Foundation model catalog:** Amazon Bedrock offers a catalog of foundation models from leading AI research organizations, such as Anthropic, Cohere, Mistral, Llama 2, and Stability. These models cover a wide range of use cases, including natural language processing, computer vision, and audio processing. Businesses can easily discover and experiment with different models through a unified interface.

- **Fine-tuning and prompt engineering tools:** Bedrock provides tools for fine-tuning foundation models on domain-specific data, enabling businesses to adapt the models to their specific use cases. The service also offers prompt engineering capabilities, allowing developers to craft effective prompts that guide the models to generate desired outputs.

- **Scalable infrastructure:** Amazon Bedrock provides scalable infrastructure for deploying and running Generative AI applications. The service automatically scales the underlying resources based on the workload, ensuring optimal performance and cost efficiency. Businesses can focus on building their applications without worrying about infrastructure management.

The use cases and examples are as follows:

- **Content creation and summarization:** The fictional company XYZ uses Amazon Bedrock to build a content creation application for their marketing team. The application leverages Bedrock's foundation models to generate product descriptions, social media posts, and blog article summaries based on structured product data and content briefs. By fine-tuning the models on XYZ's existing content, the application generates high-quality, brand-consistent content at scale, saving time and resources for the marketing team.

- **Intelligent document processing:** XYZ also integrates Amazon Bedrock with their document processing pipeline to extract insights from unstructured documents, such as contracts, reports, and customer feedback. The application uses Bedrock's foundation models to perform tasks like named entity recognition, sentiment analysis, and keyphrase extraction. The extracted insights are then fed into XYZ's SAP systems, such as SAP S/4HANA and SAP Customer Experience, enabling data-driven decision-making and process automation.

Conclusion

This chapter has explored the fundamental concepts of Generative AI within the SAP ecosystem, highlighting SAP's comprehensive approach to enterprise AI implementation. Through our examination of SAP's three-layer AI architecture, from foundation models through the AI Foundation layer to embedded AI capabilities and Joule, we have seen how SAP provides a robust framework for enterprise AI adoption.

The journey through this chapter has revealed the depth and breadth of SAP's AI capabilities. We've explored how the AI Foundation layer seamlessly integrates with partner ecosystem foundation models, ensuring robust security and governance frameworks while maintaining enterprise-grade scalability and performance. The SAP BTP reference architecture has demonstrated multiple integration patterns for existing SAP systems, showcasing the platform's flexibility in supporting various deployment scenarios across cloud and hybrid environments.

Perhaps most importantly, we've seen how these technological capabilities translate into tangible business value. Organizations implementing these solutions have achieved enhanced automation and decision-making capabilities while significantly improving user experiences through natural language interaction. The streamlined business processes and measurable productivity gains across various use cases underscore the practical impact of these implementations.

Looking ahead to *Chapter 5, Building Well-Architected Applications on SAP BTP*, we will build upon these foundational concepts to explore the practical aspects of designing and implementing effective BTP solutions and services. Our focus will shift to the critical pillars of well-architected applications, examining how to build robust and sustainable enterprise solutions.

The upcoming chapter will look at operational excellence, exploring how organizations can achieve optimal performance in their cloud implementations. We will examine key aspects, such as security measures that protect enterprise assets and ensure compliance with regulatory requirements. The discussion will extend to reliability considerations, ensuring systems maintain consistent performance under varying conditions. Performance efficiency will be a crucial topic as we explore how to optimize resource utilization while maintaining responsive systems.

Cost optimization strategies will feature prominently, providing insights into maintaining efficient operations while managing expenses effectively. Additionally, we'll address the growing importance of sustainability in enterprise architecture, examining how organizations can minimize their environmental impact through thoughtful system design and implementation.

By combining the foundational knowledge from this chapter with the architectural principles we will explore next, readers will be well-equipped to design and implement effective cloud solutions using SAP Business Technology Platform services and capabilities. The journey from understanding Generative AI concepts to implementing production-ready BTP solutions represents a crucial evolution in enterprise architecture, one that promises to deliver significant value while maintaining the highest standards of operational excellence.

Multiple choice questions

1. **What is a key component of SAP's three-layer AI portfolio?**
   a. Custom language models
   b. Hardware infrastructure
   c. Large Language Models
   d. Network optimization tools

2. **What is Retrieval-Augmented Generation (RAG) in the context of Generative AI?**
   a. A data backup system
   b. A method combining retrieval with generative models
   c. A network protocol
   d. A security framework

3. **What is the primary function of SAP AI Core?**
   a. Network management
   b. Database administration
   c. AI service and model management
   d. User interface development

4. **What is the purpose of embeddings in Generative AI?**
   a. Data encryption
   b. Network optimization
   c. Dense vector representations of data
   d. User interface design

5. **What is a key feature of SAP Joule?**
   a. Hardware management
   b. Network configuration
   c. Contextual AI assistance
   d. Database administration

6. **What is the primary purpose of the Generative AI Hub?**
   a. Network management
   b. Centralized AI development platform
   c. Database administration
   d. User interface design

7. **How does SAP integrate with Amazon Bedrock?**
   a. Hardware sharing
   b. Network optimization
   c. Foundation model access
   d. Database replication

8. **What is a key capability of SAP HANA Vector DB?**
   a. User interface design
   b. Network management

c. Efficient vector embedding storage

d. Hardware optimization

9. **What is prompt engineering in the context of Generative AI?**

a. Hardware configuration

b. Network optimization

c. Effective input design

d. Database indexing

10. **Which is a key consideration in fine-tuning Generative AI models?**

a. Hardware specifications

b. Network bandwidth

c. Domain-specific training data

d. Physical infrastructure

Answers

1. c

   Explanation: LLMs form the foundation layer of SAP's AI portfolio, incorporating both SAP-developed specialized models and partner ecosystem contributions, including models from providers like Microsoft Azure OpenAI and Anthropic's Claude.

2. b

   Explanation: RAG is a technique that combines information retrieval with generative models to produce more accurate and informative outputs by incorporating relevant information from external knowledge bases during generation.

3. c

   Explanation: SAP AI Core provides a framework for integrating and leveraging third-party LLMs and AI models, allowing customers to build, deploy, and manage AI applications across various domains.

4. c

   Explanation: Embeddings are dense vector representations of data points (words, sentences, documents) in a high-dimensional space, used to represent semantic meaning and relationships between different pieces of information.

5. c

   Explanation: SAP Joule is a digital assistant that combines artificial intelligence with business context to help users navigate applications, provide contextual support, and generate relevant content.

6. b

   Explanation: The Generative AI Hub is SAP's centralized platform for developing, deploying, and managing Generative AI applications, providing tools and services while maintaining enterprise-grade security and governance.

7. c

   Explanation: SAP integrates with Amazon Bedrock to provide access to foundation models like Claude, enabling organizations to leverage AWS's foundation models while maintaining SAP's security and governance features.

8. c

   Explanation: SAP HANA Vector DB enables efficient storage and retrieval of vector embeddings, which are essential for grounding Generative AI models and enabling contextually relevant information access.

9. c

   Explanation: Prompt engineering involves designing and crafting effective prompts or input sequences that guide the generative model to produce desired outputs, improving the quality and relevance of generated content.

10. c

    Explanation: Fine-tuning requires sufficient high-quality, domain-specific training data to adapt pre-trained models to specific use cases and improve their performance for targeted application.

CHAPTER 5
Building Well-Architected Applications on SAP BTP

Introduction

This chapter explores the fundamental principles and practices for building Well-Architected applications on SAP **Business Technology Platform** (**BTP**). As organizations increasingly move their SAP workloads to the cloud, understanding how to design and implement robust, secure, and efficient applications becomes crucial. We will examine the Well-Architected Framework's five pillars, operational excellence, security, reliability, performance efficiency, and cost optimization, and how they apply specifically to SAP BTP applications. Through practical examples and real-world scenarios, we will demonstrate how these principles can be applied to create resilient, scalable solutions that deliver business value while maintaining architectural excellence.

Structure

The chapter covers the following topics:

- Introduction to Well-Architected Framework

- Measuring success
- Building a cloud-native culture
- Cloud characteristics in Well-Architected solutions
- SAP data federation with AWS
- Well-Architected checklist for SAP BTP applications
- Examples of patterns and metrics
- Microservices architecture
- API-first design
- Edge computing

Objectives

This chapter explores the fundamental principles and practices for building Well-Architected applications on SAP BTP. As organizations increasingly move their SAP workloads to the cloud, understanding how to design and implement robust, secure, and efficient applications becomes crucial. We will examine the Well-Architected Framework's five pillars - operational excellence, security, reliability, performance efficiency, and cost optimization - and how they apply specifically to SAP BTP applications. Through practical examples and real-world scenarios, we will demonstrate how these principles can be applied to create resilient, scalable solutions that deliver business value while maintaining architectural excellence.

Introduction to Well-Architected Framework

In today's rapidly evolving digital landscape, building and maintaining enterprise applications requires more than just good coding practices. It demands a comprehensive and systematic approach to architecture that ensures applications are not only functional but also secure, reliable, cost-effective, and operationally excellent. This is where the Well-Architected Framework comes into play.

The Well-Architected Framework represents a comprehensive set of foundational concepts, design principles, and architectural best practices that guide organizations in building and operating successful cloud applications. Just as a master architect considers multiple aspects when designing a building, from the foundation and structural integrity to energy efficiency and maintenance costs, software architects must take a holistic view of their applications.

This framework is not just a set of guidelines; it is a living methodology that evolves with technology and business needs. It helps organizations ask the right questions about their architecture and make informed decisions based on proven practices and lessons learned from thousands of real-world implementations.

Five pillars of Well-Architected Framework

The pillars of the AWS Well-Architected Framework are depicted as follows.

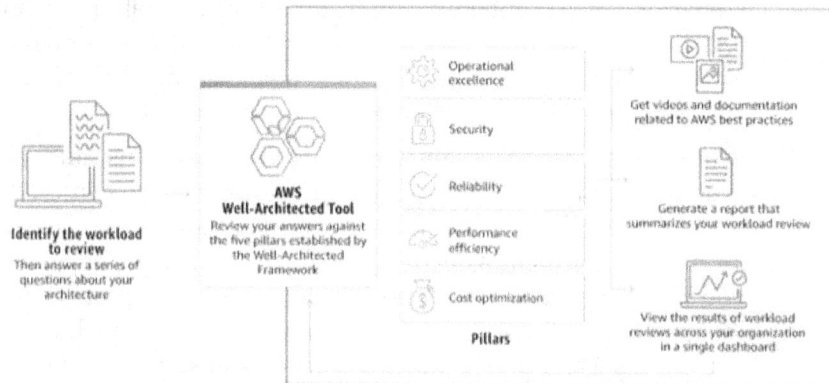

Figure 5.1: AWS Well-Architected framework

Operational excellence

Operational excellence is the foundation upon which reliable cloud operations are built. It goes far beyond simply keeping systems running; it encompasses the ability to run and monitor systems to deliver business value and to continually improve supporting processes and procedures.

At its core, operational excellence requires a deep understanding of your business objectives and how your systems support these objectives. This understanding enables you to design operations that evolve alongside your business needs while maintaining the stability and reliability your customers expect.

The key aspects of operational excellence are as follows:

- **Change management and automation**: Modern cloud environments require sophisticated change management processes. Manual changes are prone to error and do not scale effectively. Instead, organizations should embrace **infrastructure as code** (**IaC**) and automated deployment pipelines. For example, using the SAP **Cloud Application Programming** (**CAP**) Model with automated deployment scripts ensures consistent and repeatable deployments while minimizing human error.

- **Event response and incident management:** Effective operations require well-defined procedures for handling both planned and unplanned events. This includes establishing clear escalation paths, creating detailed runbooks for common scenarios, and maintaining up-to-date documentation. In an SAP BTP environment, this might involve setting up automated alerts for critical system metrics and having predefined response procedures for different types of incidents.

- **Monitoring and observability:** Modern applications must be observable, meaning they provide insights into their internal states through logs, metrics, and traces. This goes beyond basic monitoring to enable a deep understanding of system behavior and performance. For instance, implementing comprehensive logging across your SAP BTP landscape helps track user activities, system performance, and potential security issues.

Security

In today's digital landscape, security cannot be an afterthought, it must be woven into the fabric of your application's architecture from the very beginning. The security pillar focuses on protecting your information assets while delivering business value through risk assessments and mitigation strategies.

Comprehensive security framework:

- **Identity and Access Management:** A robust identity and access management system forms the cornerstone of security. In an SAP BTP environment, this means implementing the principle of least privilege, using **role-based access control** (**RBAC**), and integrating with enterprise identity providers. For example, you might use SAP Cloud Identity Services to manage user authentication and authorization across your landscape.

- **Detection and response:** Security is not just about prevention; it is also about detecting and responding to potential threats. This involves implementing comprehensive logging and monitoring solutions, setting up intrusion detection systems, and having well-defined incident response procedures. Advanced threat detection systems can help identify unusual patterns that might indicate security breaches.

- **Data protection:** Protecting data both at rest and in transit is crucial. This includes implementing encryption, managing keys securely, and ensuring proper data classification and handling. For example, sensitive data in SAP HANA databases should be encrypted, and all communications between services should use TLS encryption.

Reliability

Reliability ensures that your application performs its intended function consistently and correctly. This pillar focuses on building systems that are not just available but also resilient to various types of failures.

Building reliable systems includes:

- **System recovery:** Every system needs robust recovery mechanisms. This includes both automated recovery from common failures and manual procedures for more complex scenarios. For instance, implementing auto-scaling in your SAP BTP applications ensures they can handle varying loads without manual intervention.

- **Change management for reliability:** Changes to production systems are one of the most common sources of reliability issues. Implementing proper change management procedures, including thorough testing and controlled deployments, helps maintain system reliability. This might involve using blue-green deployment strategies or canary releases for major updates.

- **Testing and validation:** Regular testing of recovery procedures is essential. This includes not just unit tests and integration tests, but also chaos engineering practices where systems are deliberately stressed to verify their resilience.

Performance efficiency

Performance efficiency in cloud computing is about using computing resources efficiently to meet system requirements and maintaining that efficiency as demand changes. This pillar emphasizes the importance of selecting the right resources and architectures while ensuring they can scale effectively.

Achieving performance efficiency includes:

- **Resource selection and optimization:** Choosing the right computing resources is crucial for performance efficiency. This involves understanding the various options available and selecting those that best match your workload's requirements. In an SAP BTP context, this might mean choosing between different runtime environments (like Cloud Foundry or Kyma) based on your specific needs.

- **Performance monitoring and management:** Continuous monitoring of performance metrics helps identify bottlenecks and opportunities for optimization. This includes tracking response times, resource utilization, and user experience metrics. For example, using SAP Cloud ALM to monitor performance across your landscape can help identify areas needing optimization.

- **Technology evolution:** Staying current with technology changes is essential for maintaining performance efficiency. This includes evaluating new services and features as they become available and determining if they can benefit your workload. For instance, adopting new SAP HANA features or leveraging new cloud services can improve performance and efficiency.

Cost optimization

Cost optimization is about achieving business outcomes while minimizing costs. This requires a detailed understanding of spending patterns, regular cost analysis, and continuous optimization efforts.

Implementing cost optimization includes:

- **Cost awareness and tracking:** Understanding your costs starts with implementing proper cost tracking and allocation mechanisms. This includes tagging resources appropriately, setting up detailed billing reports, and regularly reviewing spending patterns. In SAP BTP, this might involve monitoring consumption units and optimizing service plan selections.

- **Resource right-sizing:** Many organizations waste resources by over-provisioning. Regular monitoring and adjustment of resource allocation ensure you are not paying for unused capacity. For example, analyzing usage patterns of SAP BTP services can help identify opportunities to downsize or upgrade services based on actual needs.

- **Cost-efficient architecture:** Architectural decisions have a significant impact on costs. This includes choosing appropriate services, implementing caching strategies, and optimizing data transfer patterns. For instance, using SAP BTP's elastic capabilities can help reduce costs during low-demand periods.

Framework implementation methodology

Successfully implementing the Well-Architected Framework requires a systematic approach that combines regular assessment, careful planning, and continuous improvement. The phases include:

- **Assessment phase:** The journey begins with a comprehensive assessment of your current architecture against each pillar of the framework. This involves a detailed analysis of your existing systems, identifying strengths and weaknesses, and understanding gaps between the current state and best practices.

- **Analysis and planning:** Based on the assessment results, develop a detailed plan for addressing identified gaps. This plan should prioritize improvements based on business impact and implementation complexity. Create a roadmap that outlines specific steps, timelines, and resources needed for implementation.

- **Implementation strategy:** Implementation should follow an iterative approach, making incremental improvements while maintaining system stability. This might involve:

  o Starting with high-priority, low-risk improvements

  o Implementing changes in test environments first

  o Conducting thorough testing before production deployment

    o   Monitoring impact of changes closely

- **Continuous review and improvement:** The Well-Architected Framework is not a one-time implementation but a continuous journey. Regular reviews help ensure your architecture continues to align with best practices and evolves with your business needs.

Measuring success

The journey of implementing a Well-Architected Framework is much like navigating a ship across vast waters. While instruments and measurements are crucial, the true measure of success extends far beyond mere numbers. Let us explore how organizations can meaningfully assess their progress across different dimensions of their cloud journey.

The quantitative story

Consider how a global retail organization measures its cloud transformation success. Their journey begins with tracking traditional metrics - system uptime, response times, and cost per transaction. But these numbers tell only part of the story. When they notice their **Mean Time to Recovery (MTTR)** dropping from hours to minutes, it is not just a statistical improvement. It represents countless customers who can complete their purchases without interruption, development teams who can sleep soundly at night, and business stakeholders who can rely on stable systems for critical operations.

Security metrics paint a similar picture. When the time to patch vulnerabilities decreases from weeks to days or even hours, it is not merely a faster response time. It represents strengthened trust from customers, reduced risk to the business, and a more confident security team. Each security incident prevented is a story of protected customer data, maintained business reputation, and uninterrupted services.

The human element

However, some of the most profound impacts resist quantification. Take, for example, a development team's journey. Before implementing Well-Architected principles, they might spend countless hours firefighting production issues. After the transformation, they find themselves innovating more, learning new skills, and delivering features faster. This improved developer experience does not show up directly in metrics, but its impact ripples through the entire organization.

The security team's evolution tells another compelling story. Rather than being seen as the **department of no**, they become trusted advisors in the development process. Their enhanced security posture is not just about fewer incidents; it is about building security into the DNA of the organization. This cultural shift, while hard to measure, fundamentally transforms how the organization approaches risk and innovation.

Business transformation

The ultimate measure of success manifests in business outcomes. When a company can launch new features in days instead of months, it is not just about deployment frequency. It is about responding to market opportunities faster, delighting customers with rapid innovations, and staying ahead of competitors. Each accelerated deployment represents potential market share gained, customer needs met, and business opportunities seized.

Consider a financial services company that reduced its operational overhead through automation and improved architecture. The real success is not just in the cost savings, but in how those resources are redirected toward innovation and customer value. The team that once spent 80% of its time maintaining systems now invests that energy in developing new customer features and exploring emerging technologies.

The ripple effect

Success in Well-Architected implementations often creates unexpected positive outcomes. A manufacturing company focusing on operational excellence finds that its improved processes not only reduce errors but also enhance employee satisfaction. Their teams, freed from repetitive operational tasks, begin innovating in ways they never had the bandwidth for before. This increased innovation leads to new product features, which in turn drive customer satisfaction and business growth.

The story of cost optimization goes beyond reduced cloud bills. When organizations implement efficient resource utilization, they often discover improved application performance, enhanced environmental sustainability, and better capacity for scaling during peak demands. Each optimization becomes a building block for future innovations.

Culture of continuous improvement

Perhaps the most significant measure of success is how an organization's culture evolves. When teams naturally consider reliability, security, and cost implications in their decisions, when they proactively seek ways to improve their architecture, and when they celebrate learning from failures as much as from successes, these cultural shifts indicate a deep, lasting transformation.

This cultural change manifests in daily operations: architects considering cost implications during design discussions, developers automatically including security controls in their code, and operations teams constantly looking for ways to improve system reliability. These behavioral changes, while difficult to quantify, often drive the most substantial long-term benefits.

The true measure of success in implementing a Well-Architected Framework lies not in any single metric or assessment but in the holistic transformation of how an organization operates, innovates, and delivers value to its customers. It is a journey of continuous improvement, where each step forward strengthens the foundation for future success. The metrics for success include:

- **Quantitative metrics:** Establish clear, measurable KPIs for each pillar. For example:
    - o **Operational excellence**: MTTR, deployment frequency
    - o **Security**: Number of security incidents, time to patch vulnerabilities
    - o **Reliability**: System uptime, error rates
    - o **Performance**: Response times, resource utilization
    - o **Cost**: Cost per transaction, resource utilization efficiency
- **Qualitative assessment:** Not all benefits can be measured numerically. Consider factors such as:
    - o Improved developer productivity
    - o Enhanced security posture
    - o Better operational visibility
    - o Increased business agility

- **Business impact:** Ultimately, success should be measured in terms of business outcomes:
  - o Faster time to market for new features
  - o Improved customer satisfaction
  - o Reduced operational overhead
  - o Better alignment with business objectives

Building a cloud-native culture

Building a cloud-native culture represents a fundamental shift in how organizations approach application development and operations. This transformation goes beyond technical changes, requiring organizations to evolve their people, processes, and tools to fully embrace cloud-native principles. The following sections explore the key aspects of this cultural transformation that organizations must address to successfully build and maintain Well-Architected applications on SAP BTP.

Transform team structures

Consider a traditional enterprise where development, operations, and security teams work in isolation. When building a cloud-native application on SAP BTP, this structure often leads to friction and delays. A real-world example would be a customer-facing portal that needs rapid updates to meet changing business needs. In a traditional setup, code changes might move slowly through different teams – developers write the code, and then hand it to operations for deployment, while security teams conduct reviews in parallel.

In a cloud-native transformation, these teams merge into cross-functional units. Each team owns its service end-to-end, from development through deployment and operations. For instance, the portal team would include developers who understand cloud infrastructure, operations specialists who can code, and security experts who are involved from day one. This team can make informed decisions about scaling, security, and deployment without lengthy handoffs or approval chains.

Adapt processes

Take the example of a critical SAP integration that needs updating. In a traditional environment, this might involve lengthy change control meetings, weekend deployment windows, and high-stress rollouts. A cloud-native approach transforms this entirely. The same update would be broken down into smaller, less risky changes. Each change goes through automated testing pipelines, can be deployed during regular business hours, and most importantly, can be rolled back instantly if issues arise.

A real-world scenario might look like this: A team needs to update an order processing integration between SAP S/4HANA and a cloud-native microservice. Instead of one big deployment, they might first update the data model, then the API interface, and finally the business logic, with each change being deployable and reversible independently. This approach reduces risk and allows for continuous improvement without disrupting business operations.

Evolve skills

The journey of a traditional SAP ABAP developer transitioning to cloud development illustrates this evolution perfectly. Rather than just learning new programming languages, they need to understand entirely new concepts. They might start by learning how their ABAP code can interact with cloud services through APIs. Then they progress to understanding cloud-native concepts like containerization, serverless functions, and distributed tracing.

For example, when developing a new customer service application, this developer would need to think beyond traditional monolithic applications. They would need to understand how to break down the application into microservices, how to handle distributed data consistency, and how to implement resilient communication patterns between services. This might mean learning how to use SAP BTP's Cloud Foundry environment, understanding event-driven architectures, and mastering new monitoring and debugging tools for distributed systems.

Change metrics and measurements

Traditional success metrics like system uptime do not tell the whole story in a cloud environment. Consider a global e-commerce platform built on SAP BTP. Instead of focusing solely on whether the system is **up** or **down**, the team monitors the entire customer journey. They track how long it takes for a customer to complete a purchase, how the system performs across different regions, and how effectively it scales during peak shopping periods.

The metrics that matter might include: The system's ability to maintain consistent response times even as user load increases, not just whether it is available. For instance, during a flash sale, the system might route traffic across multiple regions automatically to maintain performance, while traditional metrics would only show if the system was online or offline.

Cost metrics also take on new meaning in the cloud. Rather than measuring monthly infrastructure costs as a fixed expense, teams track cost per transaction or cost per customer. This allows them to optimize spending in real-time, scaling resources up or down based on actual usage patterns rather than predicted capacity needs.

A practical example would be a reporting system that traditionally ran on dedicated hardware. In the cloud, the team would monitor not just its functionality but its efficiency – how much processing power is used per report, whether resources are idle during off-hours, and how costs correlate with business value delivered. This might lead to implementing automatic scaling down during quiet periods or restructuring reporting schedules to optimize resource usage and costs.

Cloud characteristics in Well-Architected solutions

Modern cloud architecture represents a fundamental shift from traditional on-premises thinking. While the Well-Architected Framework provides the foundation for building robust solutions, understanding and embracing core cloud characteristics is crucial for successful implementation. Let us explore how these characteristics shape our approach to building enterprise solutions:

- **Evolution of enterprise architecture:** Enterprise architecture has evolved significantly with cloud adoption. Traditional approaches focused on preventing failures, maximizing hardware investments, and maintaining stable, unchanging environments. Cloud architecture, however, embraces change, expects failure, and treats infrastructure as a programmable resource. This shift fundamentally changes how we design, build, and operate enterprise applications.

- **Embracing failure as the new normal:** In traditional environments, architects designed systems to prevent failures. Hours were spent creating elaborate redundancy schemes and failover procedures. Cloud architecture takes a different approach – instead of trying to prevent failures, we design systems expecting them to occur. This is not pessimism; it is realism that leads to more resilient systems.

  Consider a global SAP analytics platform processing real-time sales data. Rather than running on carefully maintained servers with manual failover procedures, the system operates across multiple availability zones simultaneously. Each component exists in multiple instances, ready to handle failures at any level. When an availability zone experiences issues, traffic automatically redirects to healthy instances in other zones. Database connections shift to replicas, and the application continues functioning without human intervention.

- **Power of true elasticity:** Cloud elasticity goes far beyond traditional scalability. Instead of planning for peak capacity and purchasing hardware to meet potential future needs, cloud systems expand and contract automatically based on actual demand. This is not just about adding more servers – it is about intelligent resource utilization across the entire application stack.

  Take an order processing system handling variable loads throughout the day. During quiet periods, it runs on minimal infrastructure. As order volume increases, the system automatically scales not just application servers, but the entire stack – database connections expand, cache layers grow, and processing capacity increases. When demand subsides, the system scales down just as automatically, optimizing costs without sacrificing performance.

- **Serverless**: Serverless computing represents perhaps the purest form of cloud thinking. It eliminates infrastructure management entirely, allowing organizations to focus purely on business logic. This is not just about reducing operational overhead – it fundamentally changes how we approach application design.

  A document processing workflow in SAP illustrates this transformation. Traditionally, such a system would require constantly running servers to handle incoming documents.

In a serverless architecture, compute resources materialize on demand. When a document arrives, the necessary processing capacity appears automatically. Once processing is completed, these resources disappear, and costs stop accruing. The system scales from handling zero to thousands of documents per second without any infrastructure management.

- **Distributed high availability:** Cloud-native high availability transcends traditional active-passive failover models. Modern cloud applications maintain availability through distribution rather than redundancy. They run actively across multiple regions simultaneously, automatically routing users to the optimal location. Data replicates continuously across regions, ensuring consistency without sacrificing availability.

  This distributed approach extends to every aspect of the application. Database reads are spread across multiple replicas, static content is served from edge locations worldwide, and applications maintain functionality even during significant regional disruptions. The system does not just survive failures – it continues operating at full capacity despite them.

- **Network resilience and communication patterns:** Cloud networking requires rethinking communication patterns. Instead of relying on stable, high-speed connections, cloud-native applications must handle variable network conditions gracefully. This means implementing circuit breakers to prevent cascade failures, using exponential backoff for retries, and designing communication patterns that remain robust despite network instability.

  For instance, an SAP integration might use asynchronous messaging with guaranteed delivery for critical transactions, while implementing circuit breakers and fallback mechanisms for less critical operations. The network becomes an active component of the application architecture, not just a connecting layer.

- **Cost-aware architecture:** Perhaps the most transformative aspect of cloud computing is how cost becomes an integral part of architectural decisions. Every design choice has immediate cost implications. Running development environments 24/7, processing data in suboptimal regions, or maintaining unused resources directly impacts the bottom line.

This cost awareness drives architectural decisions. Should reports be generated on-demand or pre-compute during off-peak hours? Should data reside in high-performance storage or tier-based access patterns? Should processing occur near data or users? Each decision balances performance, cost, and complexity.

- **Security through automation:** Cloud security represents another fundamental shift. Instead of maintaining security through access control and perimeter defense, cloud-native applications implement security through automation and immutable infrastructure. Security policies are deployed as code, compliance checks run automatically, and infrastructure rebuilds regularly to maintain known-good states.

  These cloud characteristics do not replace the Well-Architected Framework – they enhance it. Together, they provide a comprehensive approach to building modern enterprise applications that are resilient, scalable, and cost-effective. Organizations that embrace these characteristics while following Well-Architected principles position themselves to fully leverage the benefits of cloud computing while maintaining enterprise-grade reliability and security.

Understanding and implementing these characteristics requires significant organizational change, technical skill development, and often, a complete rethinking of application architecture. However, the benefits, improved resilience, reduced costs, increased agility, and better scalability, make this transformation worthwhile for modern enterprises.

SAP data federation with AWS

Data federation between SAP systems and AWS analytics services represents a critical integration pattern for modern enterprises seeking to maximize their data value. Organizations increasingly need to combine SAP's rich business data with AWS's advanced analytics capabilities while maintaining data governance, ensuring real-time access, and optimizing costs. This use case demonstrates how to implement a Well-Architected federation solution that enables seamless data access and analytics across both platforms while adhering to key architectural principles.

Business context and challenge

In modern enterprise environments, organizations face a significant challenge: how to effectively combine and analyze data from multiple sources without creating data duplication, losing semantic context, or sacrificing real-time capabilities. Many organizations need to:

- Combine SAP business data with data stored in AWS for comprehensive analytics
- Run machine learning experiments on AWS using business data for forecasting and planning
- Maintain data governance and security while enabling real-time access
- Provide self-service analytical capabilities to business users

Traditional ETL approaches often fall short, creating data silos, increasing storage costs, and introducing data latency issues. This is where a Well-Architected data federation solution becomes crucial.

Solution overview

The solution leverages SAP Datasphere's data federation capabilities combined with AWS analytics services to create a robust, scalable, and secure data analytics platform. Let us examine how this solution embodies each pillar of our Well-Architected Framework:

- **Operational excellence implementation:**
    - o **IaC and automation:** The solution implements operational excellence through:
        - ▪ Automated deployment of AWS resources using CloudFormation or Terraform
        - ▪ Standardized configuration of SAP Datasphere connections
        - ▪ Automated monitoring and alerting setup using Amazon CloudWatch
        - ▪ Clear documentation and runbooks for operational procedures

- o **Observability and monitoring:** The solution enables comprehensive monitoring through:
  - Integration with CloudWatch for AWS service metrics
  - SAP Datasphere monitoring capabilities for federation performance
  - End-to-end request tracing for performance optimization
  - Automated alerting for threshold violations
- **Security implementation:**
  - o **Identity and access management:** Security is implemented through multiple layers:
    - AWS Secrets Manager for secure credential management
    - IAM roles and policies for fine-grained access control
    - Integration with SAP's authentication mechanisms
    - Regular key rotation policies
  - o **Data protection:** Data security is ensured through:
    - Encryption at rest using AWS KMS
    - Encryption in transit for all data transfers
    - VPC security groups and network ACLs
    - Audit logging of all data access
- **Reliability implementation**
  - o **High availability:** The solution ensures reliability through:
    - Multi-AZ deployment of AWS services
    - Automated failover capabilities
    - Load balancing for distributed requests
    - Redundant network connectivity
  - o **Error handling:** Robust error handling includes:
    - Circuit breakers for federation requests
    - Retry mechanisms with exponential backoff
    - Fallback procedures for degraded operations
    - Comprehensive error logging and monitoring

- **Performance efficiency implementation:**
  - o **Resource optimization:** Performance is optimized through:
    - Selection of appropriate instance types and services
    - Query optimization in both SAP Datasphere and AWS
    - Caching strategies for frequently accessed data
    - Network optimization for cross-platform requests
  - o **Scalability:** The solution scales efficiently through:
    - Serverless analytics with Amazon Athena
    - Auto-scaling capabilities in AWS services
    - Connection pooling for database access
    - Resource monitoring and automatic adjustments
- **Cost optimization implementation:**
  - o **Resource selection:** Costs are optimized through:
    - Use of serverless technologies where appropriate
    - Right-sizing of persistent resources
    - Automated resource scaling based on demand
    - Efficient data storage strategies
  - o **Cost monitoring:** Cost management is implemented through:
    - Detailed cost allocation tags
    - Regular cost analysis and optimization
    - Usage monitoring and trending
    - Budget alerts and controls

Reference architecture

The following is an architecture diagram showing the integration between SAP Datasphere and AWS analytics services:

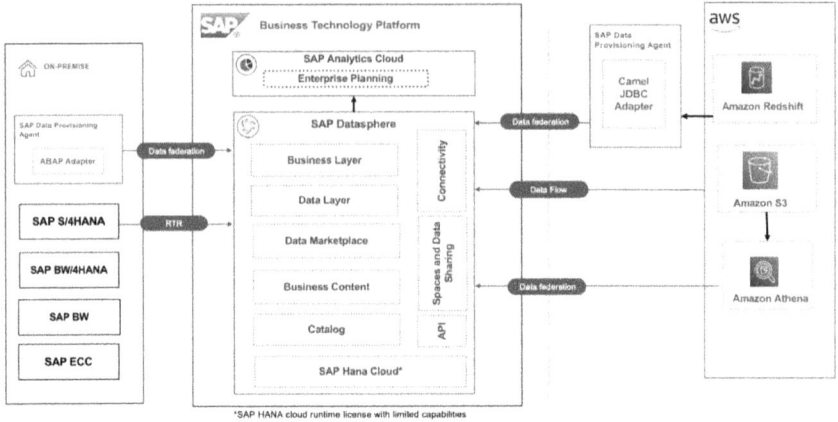

Figure 5.2: *SAP Data Federation with AWS*

The architecture consists of:

- SAP Datasphere as the semantic layer and federation engine
- Amazon S3 for data lake storage
- Amazon Athena for serverless analytics
- Amazon SageMaker for machine learning capabilities
- AWS IAM and Security services for access control

Implementation considerations

When implementing this solution, organizations should consider:

- **Data strategy:**
  - Identify which data should be federated vs. replicated
  - Define data governance policies
  - Establish data quality metrics
  - Plan for data lifecycle management
- **Integration strategy:**
  - Define integration patterns (real-time vs. batch)
  - Establish error-handling procedures
  - Plan for network connectivity
  - Design for scalability
- **Security strategy**
  - Implement least-privilege access

  o Plan for encryption and key management

  o Define audit and compliance requirements

  o Establish security monitoring procedures

Technical implementation guidelines

The technical implementation guidelines are as follows:

1. **Setting up the foundation:**

 a. AWS Environment preparation:

```
   1. Network Configuration
         - Set up VPC with appropriate subnets
         - Configure routing tables and internet
      gateways
         - Establish VPC endpoints for AWS services
         - Configure security groups and NACLs

   2. IAM Setup
         - Create service roles for Athena, S3, and
      other services
          - Configure role policies following least
      privilege
         - Set up cross-account roles if needed
          - Implement AWS Organizations for multi-
      account management
```

 b. SAP Datasphere configuration:

```
   1. Connection Setup
         - Configure Space settings
        - Set up connection parameters to AWS services
         - Configure authentication methods
         - Test connectivity and permissions

   2. Data Model Preparation
         - Define semantic layers
         - Create views and fact tables
         - Configure business context
         - Set up data access controls
```

2. **Data integration patterns:**

   a. **Real-time data access:** For real-time data access scenarios:

```
-- Example SAP Datasphere view combining real-time
data
CREATE VIEW RealTimeAnalytics AS
SELECT
    s.OrderID,
    s.CustomerID,
    a.CustomerBehavior
FROM
    "SAP_Orders" s
    JOIN "AWS_CustomerAnalytics" a
    ON s.CustomerID = a.CustomerID
WHERE
    s.OrderDate >= ADD_DAYS(CURRENT_DATE, -7)
```

   b. **Batch processing:** For large-scale data processing:

```
# AWS Glue ETL job example
def process_sap_data(glueContext, data):
    # Read SAP data
    sap_data = glueContext.create_dynamic_frame.
from_catalog(
        database="sap_federation",
        table_name="business_partners"
    )

    # Transform and enrich
    enriched_data = ApplyMapping.apply(
        frame=sap_data,
        mappings=[
            ("ID", "string", "partner_id",
"string"),
            ("NAME", "string", "partner_name",
"string"),
```

```
            ("TYPE", "string", "partner_type",
"string")
        ]
    )


    # Write to data lake
    glueContext.write_dynamic_frame.from_options(
        frame=enriched_data,
        connection_type="s3",
        path="s3://data-lake/processed/partners/",
        format="parquet"
    )
```

3. **Security implementation:**

   a. **Data encryption configuration:**

```
{
    "Version": "2012-10-17",
    "Statement": [
        {
            "Sid": "EncryptionConfig",
            "Effect": "Allow",
            "Action": [
                "kms:Encrypt",
                "kms:Decrypt",
                "kms:GenerateDataKey"
            ],
            "Resource": [
                "arn:aws:kms:region:account:key/
key-id"
            ]
        }
    ]
}
```

b. **Authentication setup:**

```
# AWS Secrets Manager integration
def get_sap_credentials():
    client = boto3.client('secretsmanager')
    response = client.get_secret_value(
        SecretId='sap-datasphere-creds'
    )
    return json.loads(response['SecretString'])
```

4. **Monitoring and observability:**

a. **CloudWatch metrics configuration:**

```
# CloudWatch dashboard configuration
Dashboard:
  Widgets:
    - type: metric
      properties:
        metrics:
          - namespace: 'SAP/Federation'
            metricName: 'QueryLatency'
            stat: 'Average'
            period: 300
        title: 'Federation Query Latency'
```

b. **Alerting setup:**

```
# CloudWatch alarm configuration
def create_performance_alarm():
    cloudwatch = boto3.client('cloudwatch')
    cloudwatch.put_metric_alarm(
        AlarmName='Federation-Latency-Alert',
        ComparisonOperator='GreaterThanThreshold',
        EvaluationPeriods=2,
        MetricName='QueryLatency',
        Namespace='SAP/Federation',
        Period=300,
        Statistic='Average',
```

```
      Threshold=1.0,
      AlarmActions=['arn:aws:sns:region:ac-
count:topic']
   )
```

5. **Performance optimization:**

   a. **Query optimization:**

```
-- Optimized federated query example
SELECT /*+ PARALLEL */
      t1.customer_id,
      t1.order_value,
      t2.customer_segment
FROM
      sap.sales_orders t1
      JOIN aws.customer_analytics t2
      ON t1.customer_id = t2.customer_id
WHERE
      t1.order_date BETWEEN ? AND ?
```

   b. **Caching strategy:**

```
# Implementation of caching layer
from aws_caching import Cache

cache = Cache(
      ttl=3600,  # Cache TTL in seconds
      max_size=1000  # Maximum cache entries
)

@cache.cached()
def get_federated_data(query_params):
      # Federated query implementation
      pass
```

6. **Cost management:**

   a. **Cost monitoring setup:**

```
# Cost monitoring implementation
def monitor_federation_costs():
```

```
client = boto3.client('ce')
response = client.get_cost_and_usage(
    TimePeriod={
        'Start': start_date,
        'End': end_date
    },
    Granularity='DAILY',
    Metrics=['UnblendedCost'],
    GroupBy=[
        {'Type': 'TAG', 'Key': 'Federation-
Workload'}
    ]
)
return response
```

7. **Operating model:**

   a. **Operational procedures:**

```
# Runbook example for federation management
Procedures:
- name: Federation Health Check
  steps:
      - Verify connectivity to SAP Datasphere
      - Check AWS service health
      - Validate data freshness
      - Monitor query performance
      - Review error logs
      - Check cost metrics

- name: Incident Response
  steps:
      - Identify affected components
      - Check error logs and metrics
      - Execute relevant recovery procedure
      - Update stakeholders
      - Document incident and resolution
```

This implementation provides a robust foundation for data federation between SAP Datasphere and AWS analytics services while adhering to Well-Architected principles. Organizations can customize and extend these components based on their specific requirements while maintaining the core architectural principles outlined.

Well-Architected checklist for SAP BTP applications

Use the following comprehensive checklist to evaluate and improve your SAP BTP applications against Well-Architected principles:

- **Operational excellence checklist:**
  - **Architecture and design:**
    - Application architecture is documented with clear component relationships
    - Service dependencies and integration points are mapped
    - Deployment architecture is defined for all environments
    - Clear separation of concerns between application layers
  - **Automation and DevOps:**
    - CI/CD pipeline is implemented for all deployment processes
    - IaC is used for environment provisioning
    - Automated testing strategy is in place
    - Deployment rollback procedures are defined and tested
  - **Monitoring and operations:**
    - Application monitoring strategy is implemented
    - **Key performance indicators (KPIs)** are defined and tracked
    - Alerting thresholds are set up and documented
    - Operational runbooks are created and maintained

- **Security checklist:**
  - **Identity and Access Management:**
    - RBAC is implemented
    - Principal of least privilege is enforced
    - Authentication mechanisms are standardized
    - Authorization flows are documented and tested
  - **Data protection:**
    - Data classification is performed
    - Encryption at rest is implemented
    - Encryption in transit is enforced
    - Data retention policies are defined and implemented
  - **Security operations:**
    - Security monitoring is in place
    - Vulnerability scanning is automated
    - Security incident response plan is documented
    - Regular security assessments are scheduled
- **Reliability checklist:**
  - **High availability:**
    - Multi-zone deployment strategy is implemented
    - Load balancing is configured appropriately
    - Auto-scaling policies are defined
    - Failover procedures are documented and tested
  - **Resilience**
    - Circuit breakers are implemented for external services
    - Retry mechanisms are in place with appropriate backoff
    - Service degradation strategies are defined
    - Data backup and recovery procedures are implemented
  - **Disaster recovery:**
    - DR strategy is documented
    - **Recovery Time Objective (RTO)** is defined

- **Recovery Point Objective (RPO)** is defined
- DR testing is performed regularly
- **Performance efficiency checklist:**
  - **Resource optimization:**
    - Instance sizing is appropriate for the workload
    - Caching strategy is implemented
    - Database performance is optimized
    - Network latency is minimized
  - **Scalability:**
    - Horizontal scaling capabilities are implemented
    - Vertical scaling limits are documented
    - Load testing is performed regularly
    - Performance bottlenecks are identified and addressed
- **Cost optimization checklist:**
  - **Resource management:**
    - Right-sizing analysis is performed regularly
    - Resource scheduling is implemented for non-production
    - Unused resources are identified and removed
    - Cost allocation tags are implemented
  - **Cost monitoring:**
    - Cost tracking mechanisms are in place
    - Budget alerts are configured
    - Cost optimization opportunities are regularly reviewed
    - License management strategy is implemented

Examples of patterns and metrics

The following sections explore proven design patterns that exemplify Well-Architected Framework principles in action. Through real-world scenarios and concrete metrics, we will examine how event-driven architectures, microservices, API-first design, and edge computing patterns can be effectively implemented on SAP BTP while maintaining architectural excellence.

Event-driven architectures

In today's digital landscape, businesses must respond to changes in real-time. Consider Global Retail Co. (a fictional company) facing challenges with its inventory management system. Their traditional request-response architecture could not keep pace with thousands of simultaneous updates from stores, online channels, and warehouses. Each system needed to communicate directly with others, creating a complex web of dependencies that became increasingly difficult to maintain and scale.

Advanced event mesh

Let us explore how implementing SAP Integration Suite, **advanced event mesh** (**AEM**), supports each pillar of the Well-Architected Framework through Global Retail Co.'s transformation journey.

Operational excellence through event-driven design

When Global Retail Co. shifted to an event-driven architecture using AEM, they transformed their operational capabilities. Instead of direct system-to-system communications, each business event became a self-contained message published to relevant subscribers. Store inventory updates, online purchases, and warehouse movements each generated events that interested systems could consume independently.

Success criteria for operational excellence:

- MTTR reduced from hours to minutes
- System dependency mapping simplified by 60%
- Deployment frequency increased from monthly to weekly
- Change failure rate decreased by 40%

Security in event-driven systems

The event-driven architecture enhanced Global Retail Co.'s security posture significantly. AEM provided fine-grained access control, ensuring that each system could only publish or subscribe to appropriate events. All event communications were encrypted, and comprehensive audit trails tracked every event's lifecycle.

Success criteria for security:

- 100% encryption coverage for event communications
- Security incident response time reduced by 50%
- Complete audit trail for all business events
- Zero unauthorized access attempts successful

Reliability through event decoupling

The move to event-driven architecture dramatically improved system reliability. When a warehouse system experienced issues, other systems continued functioning normally. Events were persisted until all interested subscribers could process them, ensuring no updates were lost during system outages.

Success criteria for reliability:

- System availability increased to 99.95%
- Zero data loss during system outages
- Recovery time reduced to under 15 minutes
- Business continuity is maintained during partial outages

Performance efficiency in event processing

AEM enabled Global Retail Co. to handle massive scale efficiently. The architecture could automatically scale event processing based on load, ensuring consistent performance during peak shopping seasons and sales events.

Success criteria for performance:

- Consistent event processing latency under 500ms
- Automatic scaling to handle 10x normal load
- 99th percentile response time under 2 seconds
- Resource utilization optimized by 40%

Cost optimization through event-driven architecture

The event-driven approach significantly optimized costs. Systems only consumed the resources needed to process their specific events, and infrastructure scaled dynamically with actual business activity.

Success criteria for cost:

- Infrastructure costs reduced by 30%
- Development costs decreased by 25%
- Maintenance effort reduced by 40%
- Resource utilization improved by 35%

Real-world implementation considerations

Global Retail Co.'s implementation followed a methodical approach:

- **First phase**: Event identification, where they began by mapping key business events across their retail operations. Each event was evaluated for business impact, frequency, and processing requirements. This careful planning ensured the event-driven architecture aligned with actual business needs.

- **Second phase:** Pilot implementation, where they started with a single business process: inventory updates. This controlled scope allowed them to validate the architecture's benefits while minimizing risk. The pilot demonstrated significant improvements in real-time inventory accuracy and system responsiveness.

- **Third phase:** Scaled deployment with proven success from the pilot, they gradually expanded the event-driven architecture across their operations. Each expansion built upon lessons learned, refining the approach for maximum benefit.

Cultural transformation

The shift to event-driven architecture required significant cultural change. Teams needed to think differently about system interactions, moving from direct control to event-based choreography. Global Retail Co. invested in training and created centers of excellence to support this transformation.

Looking forward

For organizations considering similar transformations, SAP provides several Discovery Center missions that offer guided journeys through implementing event-driven architectures. These missions provide hands-on experience with AEM and help teams understand how to apply Well-Architected principles in practice.

https://discovery-center.cloud.sap/protected/index.html#/mission-Catalog/?search=sap-integration-suite

Measuring long-term success

Global Retail Co.'s transformation delivered lasting benefits that extended beyond technical metrics:

- **Business impact:**
  - Customer satisfaction improved by 30% due to real-time inventory accuracy
  - New market entry time reduced from months to weeks
  - Innovation cycle time decreased by 50%
  - Business agility score improved by 45%
- **Organizational benefits:**
  - Team productivity increased by 35%
  - System maintenance effort reduced by 40%
  - Cross-team collaboration improved by 50%
  - Employee satisfaction scores increased by 25%

Microservices architecture

Microservices architecture has emerged as a powerful pattern for achieving these goals on SAP BTP. This architectural approach breaks down complex applications into smaller, independently deployable services, each focused on specific business capabilities.

Journey to microservices

Manufacturing Excellence Corp (a fictional company) faced growing challenges with their monolithic order processing system. As a global manufacturer of industrial equipment, they struggled with updating their system to accommodate new product lines, regional requirements, and customer-specific processes. Each change, no matter how small, required testing the entire application, leading to long deployment cycles and increased risk.

Transforming through microservices on SAP BTP

Let us explore how their transition to a microservices architecture on SAP BTP exemplified Well-Architected principles and transformed their business capabilities.

Operational excellence through service independence

The transition began by decomposing their monolithic application into discrete services based on business capabilities. Order processing, inventory management, pricing, and customer management became independent services, each owned by a dedicated team. This alignment of services with business domains created clear ownership and accountability.

Success criteria for operational excellence:

- Deployment frequency increased from monthly to daily releases
- Change failure rate decreased from 25% to 5%
- Time to restore service reduced from hours to minutes
- Developer productivity improved by 40% through focused service ownership

Security through service isolation

Each microservice implemented its own security perimeter, following the principle of least privilege. The architecture leveraged SAP BTP's security services for consistent authentication and authorization across all services while maintaining individual service-level security controls.

Success criteria for security:

- Security vulnerabilities reduced by 60%
- Compliance validation time decreased by 50%
- Attack surface reduced through service isolation
- Security incident response time improved by 70%

Reliability through service resilience

The microservices architecture enhanced system reliability by preventing cascade failures. When issues occurred in one service, others continued functioning normally. The team implemented circuit breakers, retry mechanisms, and fallback capabilities for each service.

Success criteria for reliability:

- System availability increased to 99.99%
- Fault isolation success rate at 95%
- Service recovery time under 30 seconds
- Zero unplanned downtime during deployments

Performance efficiency through granular scaling

Each microservice could scale independently based on its specific demands. The pricing service scaled up during promotions, while inventory services scaled during receiving operations. This granular control over resources significantly improved overall system efficiency.

Success criteria for performance:

- Resource utilization improved by 45%
- Peak load handling capacity increased by 300%
- Response time variance reduced by 60%
- Cost per transaction reduced by 35%

Cost optimization through resource control

The granular nature of microservices enabled precise resource allocation. Services scaled down during low-demand periods, and development teams could optimize each service independently based on its specific requirements and usage patterns.

Success criteria for cost:

- Infrastructure costs reduced by 40%
- Development costs decreased by 30%
- Maintenance costs reduced by 35%
- Resource utilization efficiency improved by 50%

Implementation journey

Manufacturing Excellence Corp's transformation followed a structured approach that others can learn from:

- **First phase**: Domain analysis:
  - o The team began with a careful analysis of their business domains, identifying natural service boundaries. They mapped business processes, data flows, and team responsibilities to inform their service decomposition strategy.
- **Second phase**: Foundation services:
  - o They identified core services that multiple business processes depended on, such as customer management and product information. These became the first candidates for migration, establishing patterns for future services.
- **Third phase**: Incremental migration:
  - o Rather than a **big bang** approach, they gradually migrated functionality to microservices. Each migration provided learning opportunities and refined their approach. The team maintained careful measurements of the before and after states to validate improvements.

Cultural shift to service ownership

The transformation required significant cultural changes. Teams shifted from component ownership to service ownership, taking full responsibility for their services from development through production operation. This **you build it, you run it** philosophy created a stronger alignment between development and business outcomes.

Manufacturing excellence corp established:

- Service ownership guidelines
- Cross-functional teams aligned with business capabilities
- DevOps practices for each service team
- Continuous learning and improvement processes

API-first design

Financial Services International (a fictional company) struggled with a common challenge in the banking industry: creating a unified digital experience across its retail banking, wealth management, and insurance divisions. Each division operated its own systems, leading to fragmented customer experiences and duplicated functionality.

Embracing API-first design on SAP BTP

Their journey to an API-first approach demonstrates how this architectural pattern supports and enhances each pillar of the Well-Architected Framework.

Operational excellence through API governance

The transformation began with establishing an API governance framework. Rather than allowing each team to create APIs independently, they implemented a design-first approach where APIs were treated as products, with clear versioning, documentation, and support processes.

Success criteria for operational excellence:

- API documentation completeness improved to 100%
- API reuse increased by 65%
- Development time reduced by 45%
- Integration issues decreased by 70%

Security through standardized API protection

API security became standardized and centralized through SAP API Management. Every API, regardless of its origin, implements consistent authentication, authorization, and threat protection measures. This standardization significantly improved their security posture.

Success criteria for security:

- API-related security incidents reduced by 80%
- Security policy compliance reached 100%

- Threat detection time improved by 60%
- Unauthorized access attempts blocked with 99.9% accuracy

Reliability through API design

The API-first approach improved system reliability by establishing clear contracts between services. Each API included comprehensive error handling, rate limiting, and circuit breaker patterns. This design-first approach prevented many common integration issues before they could occur.

Success criteria for reliability:

- API availability reached 99.99%
- Error handling coverage improved to 100%
- API response time consistency improved by 70%
- Integration-related incidents reduced by 75%

Performance efficiency through API optimization

Each API was designed with performance in mind, implementing caching strategies, pagination, and optimized data patterns. The team continuously monitored API usage patterns to identify and implement performance improvements.

Success criteria for performance:

- API response times reduced by 60%
- Cache hit ratio increased to 85%
- Bandwidth usage optimized by 50%
- Resource utilization improved by 45%

Cost optimization through API management

The API-first approach enabled precise tracking and optimization of API usage. Teams could identify underutilized APIs, optimize high-cost operations, and make data-driven decisions about API retirement or enhancement.

Success criteria for cost:

- API development costs reduced by 40%

- Maintenance costs decreased by 50%
- Infrastructure costs optimized by 35%
- Integration costs reduced by 55%

Implementation strategy

Financial Services International followed a systematic approach to its API-first transformation:

- **First phase**: API strategy development:
    - o The team began by creating a comprehensive API strategy aligned with business goals. They established API design standards, governance processes, and success metrics before beginning any implementation work.
- **Second phase**: Core API development:
    - o They identified and developed core business APIs that represented fundamental banking capabilities. These APIs became the foundation for all digital services, ensuring consistency across channels and applications.
- **Third phase:** Digital experience creation:
    - o With core APIs in place, the team rapidly developed new digital experiences. The API-first approach enabled the quick creation of mobile apps, web portals, and partner integrations, all drawing from the same underlying APIs.

Cultural evolution

The shift to API-first design required significant cultural changes. Teams needed to think differently about software development, considering APIs as products rather than just integration points. Financial Services International invested in:

- API design training and workshops
- Internal API marketplaces
- API communities of practice
- Regular API design reviews and feedback sessions

Forward-looking integration

For organizations considering an API-first approach, SAP provides detailed guidance through Discovery Center missions. These missions offer practical experience in implementing API-first design principles on SAP BTP.

https://discovery-center.cloud.sap/search/API

Measured business impact

The API-first transformation delivered significant business value:

- **Business impact:**
  - New product launch time reduced by 65%
  - Digital channel adoption increased by 75%
  - Partner integration time decreased by 80%
  - Customer satisfaction improved by 45%
- **Organizational benefits:**
  - Development efficiency increased by 60%
  - Reusable API components increased by 70%
  - Integration complexity reduced by 55%
  - Time-to-market improved by 65%

Edge computing

Smart Manufacturing Industries (a fictional company) operated multiple production facilities across three continents. Their central challenge involved processing massive amounts of sensor data from production lines while maintaining real-time response capabilities. Traditional cloud-only architectures introduced latency issues and high data transfer costs, impacting their ability to make split-second production decisions.

Implementing edge computing with SAP BTP

Their transformation to an edge computing architecture demonstrates how this pattern aligns with and strengthens each pillar of the Well-Architected Framework.

Operational excellence at the edge

The implementation began by deploying edge computing capabilities at each production facility. Instead of sending all data to the cloud, they processed critical information locally while synchronizing essential insights with their central SAP BTP environment. This approach dramatically improved their operational capabilities.

Success criteria for operational excellence:

- Machine downtime reduced by 75%
- Predictive maintenance accuracy improved to 95%
- Real-time decision-making achieved in under 50ms
- Operational visibility increased by 85%

Security through local processing

Edge computing enhances their security posture by processing sensitive production data locally. Only aggregated, anonymized data traveled to the cloud, reducing exposure of critical manufacturing information. Each edge location implemented comprehensive security controls aligned with central policies.

Success criteria for security:

- Data exposure risk reduced by 80%
- Security incident response time improved by 70%
- Compliance requirements met with 100% accuracy
- Local security controls are standardized across all sites

Reliability through distributed processing

The edge architecture significantly improved system reliability. Each facility could operate independently during network outages, maintaining critical production processes. Local processing enabled continued operation even when cloud connectivity was compromised.

Success criteria for reliability:

- Production line availability increased to 99.99%
- Network dependency impact reduced by 90%
- Recovery time from cloud outages has been reduced to zero
- Local processing uptime reached 99.999%

Performance efficiency through local processing

Edge computing dramatically improved performance by processing data where it originated. Real-time decisions happened locally, while sophisticated analytics leveraged cloud resources appropriately.

Success criteria for performance:

- Data processing latency reduced to under 10ms
- Network bandwidth usage reduced by 85%
- Cloud processing costs reduced by 60%
- Real-time analysis capabilities improved by 90%

Cost optimization through smart distribution

The edge architecture optimizes costs by processing data at the most efficient location. Critical real-time processing occurred locally, while longer-term analytics leveraged cloud economics effectively.

Success criteria for cost:

- Data transfer costs reduced by 75%
- Infrastructure costs optimized by 40%
- Operational efficiency improved by 55%
- Maintenance costs reduced by 35%

Conclusion

The Well-Architected Framework provides a comprehensive approach to building and operating applications on SAP BTP that are secure, reliable, cost-effective, and operationally excellent. As demonstrated through our examination of data federation between SAP Datasphere and AWS analytics, these principles can be practically applied to create robust enterprise solutions.

As SAP BTP continues to evolve and new capabilities become available, the Well-Architected Framework provides a consistent methodology for evaluating and implementing these changes. Organizations should:

- Establish regular architecture reviews using the framework
- Maintain and update their Well-Architected checklists

- Train teams on framework principles and implementation
- Automate compliance with framework principles where possible
- Share learnings and best practices across teams

By following these guidelines and continuously evaluating against the Well-Architected Framework, organizations can build and maintain SAP BTP applications that are reliable, secure, cost-effective, and operationally excellent while meeting their business objectives.

Multiple choice questions

1. **What are the five pillars of the Well-Architected Framework?**

   a. Design, Development, Testing, Deployment, Maintenance

   b. Security, Performance, Cost, Reliability, Operations

   c. Operational excellence, Security, Reliability, Performance efficiency, Cost optimization

   d. Planning, Building, Testing, Deploying, Monitoring

2. **What is a key aspect of operational excellence in the Well-Architected Framework?**

   a. Maximum resource allocation

   b. Automation and event response

   c. Highest performance settings

   d. Maximum security controls

3. **In the context of reliability, what is the significance of distributed processing?**

   a. Increased costs

   b. Enhanced security

   c. Independent operation during outages

   d. Better user interface

4. **What is a key characteristic of event-driven architectures in SAP BTP?**

   a. Synchronous processing only

   b. Decoupled system communications

c. Single point of failure

d. Fixed resource allocation

5. **What role does SAP Advanced Event Mesh (AEM) play in architecture?**

a. Database management

b. User interface design

c. Event-driven messaging

d. Hardware optimization

6. **What is a key consideration in API-first design?**

a. Hardware specifications

b. Network topology

c. API lifecycle management

d. Database selection

7. **What is the primary purpose of edge computing in SAP architectures?**

a. User interface enhancement

b. Local data processing

c. Database optimization

d. Network security

8. **What is a key aspect of cost optimization in Well-Architected applications?**

a. Maximum resource allocation

b. Continuous cost monitoring

c. Fixed infrastructure sizing

d. Manual scaling processes

9. **How does the Well-Architected Framework address security?**

a. Through hardware upgrades

b. Network protocols only

c. Comprehensive security layers

d. Single security tool

10. **What is a key characteristic of performance efficiency in the framework?**

    a. Maximum resource allocation

    b. Fixed infrastructure size

    c. Efficient resource utilization

    d. Manual scaling only

Answers

1. c

   Explanation: The Well-Architected Framework consists of five fundamental pillars that guide organizations in building and operating successful cloud applications: operational excellence, security, reliability, performance efficiency, and cost optimization.

2. b

   Explanation: Operational excellence emphasizes the automation of processes and effective event response procedures, including establishing clear escalation paths, creating detailed runbooks, and maintaining up-to-date documentation.

3. c

   Explanation: Distributed processing significantly improves system reliability by allowing each facility to operate independently during network outages, maintaining critical production processes even when cloud connectivity is compromised.

4. b

   Explanation: Event-driven architectures enable decoupled system communications where each business event becomes a self-contained message published to relevant subscribers, allowing systems to operate independently.

5. c

   Explanation: SAP **Advanced Event Mesh (AEM)** supports event-driven architecture by providing a framework for integrating and leveraging event-based messaging across applications and systems.

6. c

   Explanation: API-first design emphasizes comprehensive API lifecycle management, including versioning, documentation, and support processes, treating APIs as products with clear governance frameworks.

7. b

   Explanation: Edge computing enables processing data where it originates, reducing latency and bandwidth usage while enabling real-time decision-making at the edge of the network.

8. b

   Explanation: Cost optimization involves continuous monitoring and analysis of resource usage, implementing automated controls, and ensuring resources are properly sized based on actual needs.

9. c

   Explanation: The framework addresses security through multiple layers, including identity and access management, data protection, detection and response capabilities, and comprehensive security controls.

10. c

    Explanation: Performance efficiency focuses on using computing resources efficiently to meet system requirements and maintaining that efficiency as demand changes, including appropriate resource selection and optimization.

Join our book's Discord space

Join the book's Discord Workspace for Latest updates, Offers, Tech happenings around the world, New Release and Sessions with the Authors:

https://discord.bpbonline.com

CHAPTER 6
Managing Application Security and Costs

Introduction

With agile development and deployment, applications running across cloud infrastructure and on-premises security become of utmost importance to safeguard your data and processes. Learn how to secure your application development at different layers to protect against vulnerabilities and the exposure of data.

Structure

The chapter covers the following topics:

- Understanding security paradigm
- Shared responsibility model
- Understanding security in RISE with SAP
- Customer connectivity in RISE with SAP PCE
- Introducing Security on SAP Business Technology Platform
- SAP Business Technology Platform connectivity

Objectives

Upon completing this chapter, you will gain a foundational understanding of the security paradigm within the context of SAP solutions, specifically focusing on the shared responsibility model and its implications. You will learn to navigate the security landscape of RISE with SAP, differentiating security aspects managed by SAP and those incumbent upon the customer. Furthermore, the chapter will equip you with knowledge regarding customer connectivity options within the RISE with SAP **Private Cloud Edition** (**PCE**). Finally, you will be introduced to the security principles and connectivity mechanisms inherent in the SAP **Business Technology Platform** (**BTP**), providing a comprehensive overview of securing and connecting within the broader SAP ecosystem.

Understanding security paradigm

In recent conversations with a majority of our customers, it has become evident that security stands as a critical pillar within their strategic initiatives. As these organizations progressively shift towards adopting and developing more cloud-native applications, the imperative to effectively manage security and compliance has intensified. This growing focus is not only due to the inherent security challenges associated with cloud computing but also because of the increasing complexity and regulatory scrutiny that comes with digital transformation. Consequently, as customers deepen their engagement with cloud technologies, the urgency to implement robust security frameworks and compliance measures escalates. This involves not only protecting their digital assets from cyber threats but also ensuring that their cloud-native solutions adhere to stringent industry standards and regulations. The drive towards enhancing security and compliance reflects a broader recognition of their pivotal role in safeguarding the integrity, availability, and confidentiality of critical business operations in the cloud environment.

The security paradigm tailored for SAP applications within cloud environments embodies an extensive and meticulously structured framework, specifically engineered to safeguard data, applications, and infrastructures operating in cloud ecosystems. This paradigm is methodically constructed upon a multifaceted security architecture, incorporating several layers of defense mechanisms to effectively counteract a wide spectrum of potential threats and vulnerabilities.

Such a comprehensive approach is pivotal in maintaining the integrity, confidentiality, and availability of business-critical SAP systems, which are integral to the seamless operation of enterprise-level functions and processes.

At the heart of this security paradigm are several key components, each playing a crucial role in fortifying the security posture of SAP applications in the cloud:

- **In-depth defense strategies:** In-depth defense strategies entail the adoption of a layered security methodology, fundamentally designed to establish a comprehensive shield against potential cyber threats. This strategic framework guarantees the implementation of multiple defensive measures at various levels within the system's architecture, significantly diminishing the likelihood of a security breach stemming from a single vulnerability. By integrating a series of protective barriers, each designed to counter specific types of threats, this approach not only fortifies the security perimeter around critical assets but also ensures that should one layer be compromised, additional layers of defense are in place to thwart the advancement of malicious activities.

- **Comprehensive data protection measures:** They are pivotal to safeguarding sensitive information within an organization's digital ecosystem. These measures extend beyond basic security protocols to encompass a wide array of strategies and technologies designed to secure data across all stages of its lifecycle. Central to this approach is the encryption of data both at rest and in transit, ensuring that sensitive information remains incomprehensible and secure from unauthorized interception or access. Encryption at rest protects data stored on physical or virtual storage systems, while encryption in transit secures data as it moves across networks, between applications and databases, or as it's shared externally.

- **Cloud infrastructure security:** Securing cloud infrastructure is essential for protecting digital assets and operations hosted in the cloud. This thorough approach involves implementing various strategic actions and employing cutting-edge technologies to strengthen the core components of cloud platforms, guarding them against a wide range of vulnerabilities and security threats. The focus on the underlying infrastructure of the cloud is meant to establish a robust and secure foundation that supports the safe and dependable functioning of applications, data, and services. Through this concerted effort, organizations strive to ensure that their cloud environment is a fortress, capable of withstanding security challenges and providing a trustworthy platform for their digital endeavors.

- **Regulatory compliance and governance**: It is crucial to maintain cloud infrastructure in strict alignment with pertinent industry norms, legal regulations, and established best practices, including but not limited to the **General Data Protection Regulation (GDPR)**, the **Health Insurance Portability and Accountability Act (HIPAA)**, or the **Payment Card Industry Data Security Standard (PCI-DSS)**. This comprehensive approach necessitates the implementation of a robust framework for regular audits and compliance evaluations to ensure all aspects of the cloud environment are scrutinized for adherence. Additionally, it involves the strategic adoption of security controls and protocols designed not just to meet the basic regulatory demands but to exceed them, thereby establishing a higher standard of data protection and operational integrity. This proactive stance on compliance helps in mitigating risks, enhancing data security, and ensuring trust in cloud-based operations among stakeholders.

Shared responsibility model

Cloud security is governed by a shared responsibility model, which delineates the security obligations between the **cloud service provider (CSP)** and the customer to cover different dimensions of security management. This collaborative approach ensures that while the CSP focuses on securing the infrastructure and network components that make up the cloud environment, the customer is responsible for safeguarding their data, managing access controls, and protecting their applications, including SAP applications. Furthermore, the security obligations evolve with the RISE with SAP and GROW with SAP frameworks for SAP deployment. As explored in earlier chapters, RISE with SAP represents a managed Private Cloud offering by SAP, where SAP takes charge of everything from the SAP client 000, to the operating system and downwards, altering the distribution of security responsibilities. Overall security is a shared responsibility between the CSP and the customer as follows:

- **Cloud service provider responsibilities**: The CSP is tasked with the protection of the cloud infrastructure, which includes ensuring the physical security of data centers, safeguarding network and hardware systems, and maintaining the security of the core cloud software.

- **Customer responsibilities**: The customer holds the responsibility for the security of their SAP applications and data and the management of access permissions. This duty involves overseeing user identities and access rights, implementing data encryption strategies, and ensuring the security of application interfaces.

This shared model ensures that while the CSP creates a secure cloud infrastructure, customers have the flexibility and responsibility to tailor the security of their SAP applications according to their specific needs and regulatory requirements. This collaborative approach not only optimizes the security of cloud-based SAP applications but also delineates clear boundaries of responsibility, ensuring that both the CSP and the customer play active roles in maintaining a secure cloud computing environment.

Understanding security in RISE with SAP

In the preceding discussions, we explored the transformative impact of RISE with SAP on the deployment methodologies of SAP applications and modules. This chapter aims to delve deeper into the architectural nuances of security frameworks within the RISE with SAP, specifically focusing on its **Private Cloud Edition (PCE)**. The adoption of SAP Business Technology Platform by customers marks a significant shift towards mitigating technical debt. This strategic move not only maintains the integrity of the core system but also leverages advanced cloud-native tools and services to address complex business challenges effectively.

The comprehensive RISE with SAP package includes several key components: the SAP S/4HANA Cloud Suite, which serves as the digital core; the SAP Business Technology Platform Consumption, which offers a flexible model for accessing a wide range of SAP services; the SAP Business Network Starter Pack, facilitating seamless collaboration across business networks; and the SAP Business Process

Intelligence, providing insights and analytics to optimize business processes.

Security and compliance are given top priority, considering the critical nature of the tasks handled by both the SAP S/4HANA Cloud, Private Edition, and the SAP Business Technology Platform. These platforms are integral to managing mission-critical business operations, orchestrating integration flows, conducting analytics, enhancing business processes, and fostering application development. Ensuring robust security measures and compliance with regulatory standards is essential to safeguard sensitive data and maintain the trust of stakeholders involved in these processes.

Adhering to the shared responsibility model, customers have the flexibility to select their preferred cloud provider, such as **Amazon Web Services (AWS)**, for deploying RISE with SAP and the SAP Business Technology Platform. This model delineates the responsibilities, where AWS manages the data center, infrastructure, network, and more, and SAP assumes the role of overseeing the platform and technical managed services. In contrast, customers retain control over the security of their data and applications, tailoring protection measures to suit the unique needs of their businesses and users.

This collaborative approach allows for a more customized and secure deployment, enabling businesses to leverage the strengths of their chosen cloud provider's infrastructure while benefiting from SAP's expertise in managing the platform's technical aspects. Customers are thus empowered to focus on securing their business-critical data and applications, implementing robust security protocols and measures that align with their specific operational requirements and regulatory compliance obligations. This shared responsibility framework ensures a balanced distribution of duties, optimizing the security and efficiency of cloud deployments for businesses leveraging RISE with SAP and the SAP Business Technology Platform.

The SAP S/4HANA Cloud, Private Edition, represents a uniquely **single-tenant** environment, distinguished as **private** owing to its deployment within a logically segregated **Virtual Network (VNET)** or **Virtual Private Cloud (VPC)**. This setup is akin to providing a dedicated network container exclusively for a single customer's use. Such an environment ensures that network services, including gateways, proxies, DNS services, **load balancers (LB)**, and **web application firewalls (WAF)**, along with application and HANA instances, are solely allocated to one customer. These resources are further personalized through the assignment of Private IP Addresses, enhancing the security and customization of the service.

The configuration of this VNET takes place within customer-specific, dedicated accounts at a chosen cloud provider, such as AWS, though it remains under the ownership and management of SAP. This arrangement offers a blend of privacy and exclusivity, as customers benefit from a network environment that is tailored to their specific needs, while still leveraging the robust infrastructure and management expertise provided by SAP. Such a model not only enhances security by providing a dedicated and isolated environment but also allows for greater control and customization, enabling businesses to optimize their SAP S/4HANA Cloud deployment in alignment with their specific operational requirements and strategic objectives.

Meeting security requirements

The S/4HANA Private Cloud is built on several foundational elements designed to meet the SAP landscape's security and compliance needs for customers. It operates within a VPC that provides logical isolation, creating a bespoke application environment exclusively for the customer. This configuration incorporates the allocation of Private IP Addresses that are reserved for the customer, thereby bolstering both security and the ability to tailor solutions. Additionally, a secure and private link is established from the customer's location to the SAP Private Managed Environment. This dedicated environment is hosted on a customer-specific VPC within a cloud infrastructure provided by a major CSP, such as AWS. This setup facilitates a secure, direct exchange of data and applications between the customer and SAP's managed services, ensuring optimal security, performance, and the ability to customize. This strategic approach not only meets the unique demands of customers but also lays down a strong and secure foundation for deploying their S/4HANA Private Cloud.

SAP assumes comprehensive operational and management responsibilities, which encompass a wide range of services to ensure the smooth and secure running of the PCE. These responsibilities include:

- **Infrastructure Management**: SAP oversees the entire infrastructure hosted on AWS, managing the allocation of resources, scaling, performance optimization, and ensuring high availability to meet the dynamic needs of businesses.

- **OS management**: This involves the administration of the operating systems on which the applications run, including updates, patches, and security measures to maintain system integrity and reliability.

- **DB management**: SAP handles all aspects of database management, ensuring efficient data storage, retrieval, and security. This includes performance tuning, backup and recovery processes, and database updates to optimize data handling and storage.

- **Orchestration and account configurations**: SAP manages the orchestration of services and configurations of accounts to streamline processes, automate deployments, and integrate services seamlessly for enhanced operational efficiency.

- **SAP AS basis management**: This includes the administration of the SAP Application Server Basis, which is the foundation for SAP applications. It involves monitoring system performance, managing user access, and ensuring the stable operation of SAP systems.

- **Security monitoring:** SAP actively monitors the cloud environment for potential security threats, implementing proactive measures to protect data and applications from unauthorized access and cyberattacks.

- **Audit and compliance**: SAP conducts regular audits and ensures compliance with industry standards and regulations, maintaining a strong governance framework to meet legal and regulatory requirements and uphold data integrity and privacy.

By taking on these responsibilities, SAP provides businesses with a robust and secure cloud environment, enabling them to focus on their core activities while benefiting from SAP's expertise in managing complex cloud landscapes. This comprehensive approach to operational and management responsibilities ensures that the SAP Private Cloud Edition is optimized for performance, security, and compliance, offering a reliable and efficient platform for enterprise applications.

Customer connectivity in RISE with SAP PCE

Customers frequently inquire about the specifics of setting up their RISE account, particularly the configuration processes for the VPC, security groups, and the secure connection protocols to their RISE with SAP environment hosted on cloud platforms such as AWS. They are keen to understand the steps involved in establishing and managing secure connectivity and how this extends across Business Technology Services. Additionally, there is a significant interest in how they can integrate and maintain secure connections to their non-SAP landscapes, which are hosted within their own accounts on a cloud provider platform like AWS.

To expand on these queries, the setup process for a RISE account involves several key steps, starting with the creation and configuration of a VPC. This VPC acts as a dedicated network within AWS, isolated from other networks, ensuring that customers' SAP environments are secure and isolated from external threats. Within this VPC, security groups are meticulously configured to define the inbound and outbound traffic rules, ensuring that only authorized traffic can access the network, thereby enhancing the security of the SAP environment.

Connecting securely to the RISE with the SAP environment involves utilizing secure connection methods such as VPNs or AWS Direct Connect, providing encrypted and direct connections to the cloud environment. This ensures that data in transit between the customer's on-premise environments and the RISE with SAP environment on AWS is protected against interception and unauthorized access.

When it comes to managing security and connectivity across Business Technology Services, customers are provided with tools and services that help monitor and manage security policies, access controls, and connectivity options. This comprehensive approach ensures that all aspects of the SAP environment, from applications to data, are secured against cyber threats while maintaining high availability and performance.

For connectivity requirements to customers' non-SAP landscapes hosted on their accounts within AWS, the setup includes configuring peering connections or transit gateways. These configurations allow for seamless and secure communication between the SAP and non-

SAP environments, enabling businesses to operate a cohesive and integrated IT landscape across different cloud resources.

Virtual private connection

Customers have the option to establish a secure connection to their dedicated VNET in the cloud using an IPSec-based **Site-to-Site** (**S2S**) VPN over the Internet. This method enables a secure tunnel between the customer's on-premises network and their cloud network, ensuring encrypted data transmission and safeguarding against unauthorized access. However, it is important to note that the **Point-to-Site** (**P2S**) VPN scenario, which typically allows individual devices to connect to the cloud network over the internet, is not supported in this context.

The configuration of a VPN largely depends on the cloud platform where the deployment is hosted. Each cloud provider, such as AWS, has specific requirements and guidelines for setting up VPN connections. These guidelines are detailed in the cloud provider's official documentation and should be consulted to ensure compliance and optimal configuration. Customers are responsible for verifying the compatibility of their VPN devices with the chosen cloud provider's environment. This entails checking the supported VPN device list for the specific cloud provider to ensure seamless integration and functionality.

Expanding further, the choice of an IPSec-based S2S VPN connection facilitates a robust and secure method for enterprises to extend their on-premise networks into the cloud. This setup is crucial for businesses that require a consistent and secure network connection for accessing cloud resources, applications, and services as if they were located within their own data center. The need to consult the cloud provider's documentation and verify VPN device compatibility underscores the importance of a tailored approach to network security and connectivity in cloud environments. Businesses must undertake due diligence to understand the technical and security implications of their cloud network configurations, leveraging the detailed guidance provided by cloud providers to optimize their cloud connectivity and security posture.

Dedicated private network

For accessing productive workloads, it is highly recommended to establish a dedicated private connection that includes redundancy to guarantee quality of service and higher levels of availability. This approach is crucial for businesses that rely on cloud services for critical operations, as it ensures a stable and reliable network pathway, minimizing the risk of downtime and maximizing performance.

Solutions provided by cloud infrastructure providers, like AWS Direct Connect, offer a means to set up such dedicated network connections. AWS Direct Connect, for example, allows for the establishment of a private connection between an organization's data center and AWS infrastructure. This bypasses the public internet, providing a more secure, consistent, and low-latency connection, which is ideal for handling sensitive and high-volume workloads with stringent performance requirements.

Additionally, information regarding edge locations and networking partners, which are essential for configuring and optimizing these connections, is readily available in the documentation provided by the cloud providers. Edge locations play a vital role in reducing latency by routing traffic through the nearest point of presence, while networking partners can facilitate the physical connection from an organization's premises to the cloud provider's network.

Expanding on this, leveraging dedicated private connections like AWS Direct Connect not only enhances network performance but also contributes to a more predictable operational environment. By securing a direct path to the cloud, organizations can better manage their network resources, tailor their bandwidth requirements, and implement comprehensive redundancy strategies. These strategies are paramount for maintaining uninterrupted access to cloud resources, especially for applications that demand real-time data access and high-throughput processing.

For organizations moving significant portions of their IT infrastructure to the cloud, investigating and utilizing the networking solutions offered by their chosen cloud provider is a critical step. It ensures that their cloud-based applications and services run smoothly, securely, and without interruption, thus supporting continuous operational excellence.

Introducing Security on SAP Business Technology Platform

The **SAP Business Technology Platform** (**SAP BTP**) stands as a cornerstone within SAP's suite of solutions, designed to assist customers in maintaining a streamlined and efficient core while facilitating the modernization of their SAP landscape. In my interactions, the topic of security within SAP BTP has been a recurrent point of discussion, especially as customers begin to employ SAP BTP for their mission-critical business processes.

As organizations increasingly rely on SAP BTP to drive their crucial operations, the emphasis on ensuring robust security measures has never been more pronounced. This focus stems from the platform's role in integrating and extending applications, managing databases, and harnessing advanced technologies, all of which are pivotal in supporting the seamless and secure execution of business functions.

In expanding on the security aspect of SAP BTP, it is important to understand that it offers a comprehensive security framework designed to protect data, applications, and services across the cloud and hybrid environments. This framework encompasses a variety of security features, including identity and access management, data protection and privacy, network and application security, and compliance and risk management. Each of these components plays a vital role in fortifying the platform against potential threats and vulnerabilities, thereby ensuring that customers can leverage SAP BTP for their mission-critical processes with confidence.

Moreover, as customers navigate their digital transformation journeys, the ability of SAP BTP to provide a secure and resilient foundation becomes crucial in enabling innovation and growth while safeguarding sensitive information and processes. The platform's security capabilities are continuously evolving, aimed at addressing the dynamic nature of cyber threats and meeting the stringent demands of regulatory compliance.

Therefore, when discussing SAP BTP with customers, it is imperative to highlight not only its role in driving business modernization but also its commitment to delivering a secure environment that customers can depend on for their most critical operations.

At the heart of navigating and utilizing the comprehensive capabilities of SAP BTP is the SAP BTP cockpit. This centralized dashboard serves as the primary portal through which users can access their accounts and applications, offering an intuitive interface for the management of various activities related to these resources. From the SAP BTP cockpit, users can easily deploy and scale applications, manage service integrations, monitor performance and usage metrics, and configure security settings, among other tasks. This central point of entry simplifies the complexity of managing applications across multiple cloud environments, making it easier for businesses to adopt and optimize their use of cloud resources.

The foundation of securing the SAP BTP begins with a deep understanding of its organizational structure, specifically through the global account, directory, and sub-account hierarchy. This structure is pivotal in ensuring that the appropriate level of access is meticulously granted to the right individuals who are involved in the development and deployment processes on the SAP BTP platform. By comprehensively grasping this hierarchical framework, organizations can implement precise access control measures, aligning with best practices in security and compliance.

Expanding on this, the global account serves as the top-level entity in the SAP BTP architecture, offering a consolidated view and management capability over all associated resources and services. Beneath the global account, directories provide a way to organize and manage related projects and teams, serving as containers that group together multiple sub-accounts for better organization and governance. Sub-accounts act as individual containers that house specific applications, services, and resources, allowing for fine-grained control over access and permissions at a more granular level.

Understanding this layered architecture is crucial for implementing a robust security strategy on the SAP BTP platform. It enables administrators to tailor access rights and permissions with precision, ensuring that developers, operators, and other stakeholders have only the access necessary to perform their roles, adhering to the principle of least privilege. This approach not only enhances the security posture of the platform but also facilitates compliance with internal and external regulations by providing a clear and auditable structure for access management.

Furthermore, by leveraging this hierarchical model, organizations can streamline the development and deployment workflows on the SAP

BTP platform, ensuring that security and compliance are integrated into every stage of the process. This structured approach to access and permission management is a critical step in safeguarding sensitive data and applications, mitigating the risk of unauthorized access, and enhancing the overall security of the SAP BTP environment.

Securing BTP connectivity to other cloud infrastructure and services or on-premise landscape is very important. SAP BTP Connectivity is a key component designed to empower SAP BTP applications with the capability to securely interact with remote services, whether they are hosted on the Internet or within on-premise environments. This essential feature plays a pivotal role in bridging the gap between cloud-based applications and external services, ensuring seamless integration and secure data exchange. The functionality of SAP BTP Connectivity extends across several dimensions to support a wide range of integration scenarios:

- **Subaccount-specific configuration using destinations**: SAP BTP Connectivity enables the configuration of application connections at the subaccount level through the use of destinations. This feature allows for tailored connection settings for each application, ensuring that connectivity is optimized and secure based on the specific needs and contexts of different applications within a subaccount.

- **Java API for consuming remote services:** To facilitate the development process, SAP BTP Connectivity offers a Java API that application developers can leverage to easily consume remote services. This API simplifies the integration of external services into SAP BTP applications, enabling developers to focus on building robust and feature-rich applications without worrying about the complexities of establishing secure connections to remote services.

- **Integration with on-premise systems using the Cloud connector**: For organizations looking to extend their on-premise systems to the cloud, SAP BTP Connectivity provides a seamless solution through the Cloud connector. This tool allows for the establishment of secure connections to on-premises systems, enabling cloud applications to access and interact with data and services hosted internally within an organization's network.

- **Secure tunneling for on-premises networks**: SAP BTP Connectivity also supports the creation of a secure tunnel from an organization's on-premise network to applications hosted on SAP BTP. This capability ensures that data transmitted between on-premises systems and the cloud is securely encapsulated, while also providing organizations with full control and auditability over what information and services are exposed to the cloud. This level of control and security is crucial for maintaining compliance with regulatory requirements and safeguarding sensitive business data.

Through these features, SAP BTP Connectivity not only enhances the interoperability between cloud applications and external services but also upholds stringent security standards to protect data and maintain the integrity of business operations. By facilitating secure and efficient connections, SAP BTP Connectivity enables organizations to fully leverage the power of SAP BTP in extending their business processes and services to the cloud, fostering innovation and driving digital transformation.

SAP Business Technology Platform connectivity

SAP Business Technology Platform (BTP) offers a robust set of services designed to help organizations seamlessly integrate, manage, and optimize their data across various systems and applications. These connectivity options and patterns define how systems communicate— whether in on-premise, cloud, or hybrid environments. These connectivity patterns are crucial for ensuring smooth data flow, high system performance, and robust security. BTP supports various integration scenarios, including real-time data exchange, batch processing, API-based communication, and event-driven architectures. In this section, we will explore the different connectivity patterns and options available within SAP BTP, providing you with insights into how they can be applied in diverse business contexts and guiding you in selecting the most effective approach for your integration strategy.

Introducing SAP PrivateLink Service

As mentioned earlier, security holds paramount importance for customers leveraging the SAP BTP services to innovate and revolutionize their SAP applications and business processes. Recognizing this critical need, the SAP Private Link service offers a robust solution by facilitating a private connection between selected services on the SAP BTP and specific services within your own **infrastructure-as-a-service (IaaS)** provider accounts. This is achieved by harnessing the private link capabilities offered by partner IaaS providers like AWS.

The essence of the SAP Private Link service is its ability to enable secure access to cloud services through private network connections, effectively bypassing the public internet. This approach significantly minimizes the risk of data exposure and unauthorized access, ensuring that data transfer occurs within a secure and controlled environment. It not only enhances security but also improves performance by reducing latency and potential bottlenecks associated with public internet data transfer.

Expanding on this, the integration of SAP Private Link with your IaaS provider's infrastructure creates a seamless and secure bridge between your cloud resources and the SAP ecosystem. This connectivity model is crucial for enterprises looking to maintain the integrity and confidentiality of their data while leveraging cloud scalability and flexibility. It allows for a more efficient data flow, enabling businesses to optimize their cloud investments and ensure that their SAP applications and business processes are both agile and secure.

Moreover, the utilization of private links underscores a strategic move towards a more secure cloud architecture, where data sovereignty and compliance with regulatory requirements are effortlessly managed. By facilitating direct, private connections, companies can better align their IT infrastructure with governance policies and compliance standards, ensuring that their digital transformation journey is both innovative and secure.

In summary, the SAP Private Link service represents a key component in the modernization and transformation strategy of SAP-centric enterprises. It provides a secure, efficient, and compliant pathway for businesses to connect their critical applications and services, empowering them to harness the full potential of the SAP Business Technology Platform while maintaining the highest standards of security and performance.

In a collaborative effort, AWS and SAP introduced SAP PrivateLink for AWS, aimed at enabling customers to securely harness specific and crucial services from the extensive set of over 200+ offerings provided by AWS. This initiative offers customers the flexibility to select key AWS services that can be seamlessly integrated with SAP BTP services.

The goal is to address their unique business challenges while ensuring that both the connection to these services and the transfer of data remain secure.

Realize secure connectivity

This collaboration signifies a strategic move to enhance the interoperability and security of cloud services, facilitating a smoother and more secure integration between AWS's powerful cloud infrastructure and the comprehensive suite of applications and services offered by the SAP BTP. By narrowing down the focus to selected AWS services, customers can tailor their cloud infrastructure to meet specific business needs, leveraging state-of-the-art AWS technologies in concert with SAP's enterprise-grade application and data management capabilities.

Furthermore, this partnership underscores a commitment to providing a secure cloud environment where customers can confidently navigate their digital transformation journeys. The use of SAP PrivateLink for AWS ensures that data does not traverse the public internet, thereby reducing exposure to potential security threats and vulnerabilities. This secure integration framework empowers businesses to innovate and scale while maintaining strict data privacy and security protocols.

In essence, the launch of SAP PrivateLink on AWS marks a significant milestone in cloud computing, offering businesses a robust platform for leveraging the best of both AWS and SAP technologies. It enables enterprises to drive efficiency, innovation, and security in their operations, providing a solid foundation for solving complex business challenges in today's digital landscape.

Cost optimization measures

In recent conversations with customers in almost every segment and industry, cost optimization and predictability stand out as significant considerations for businesses transitioning to the cloud. This shift from **capital expenditure (CapEx)** to **operational expenditure (OpEx)** models marks a fundamental change in how organizations budget and manage their IT expenses. With the cloud's pay-as-you-go pricing structure, companies are actively seeking strategies to enhance their financial efficiency and gain better control over their cloud spending.

Expanding on this, the move to OpEx spending allows organizations to scale their resources up or down based on demand, offering unprecedented flexibility compared to the traditional CapEx model, which requires substantial upfront investment in hardware and software. However, this flexibility also introduces complexity in budgeting and cost management, as cloud costs can fluctuate significantly with changes in usage patterns.

Moreover, organizations are investing in cloud financial management skills and practices, often referred to as FinOps, to ensure that their cloud investments are aligned with their business objectives. FinOps brings together technology, business, and finance professionals to drive cost efficiency through collaborative decision-making and shared accountability.

As cloud technology continues to evolve, staying vigilant about cost optimization and predictability will remain crucial for businesses. By embracing a culture of continuous improvement and leveraging the right tools and practices, companies can harness the power of the cloud in the most financially sustainable way.

A few areas of continuous effort and concerns from customers are:

- **Right sizing of landscape**: Resource right-sizing is an ongoing cycle of assessment and modification of cloud resources to ensure they are in perfect harmony with an organization's changing needs. This strategy is pivotal in achieving an optimal equilibrium between operational performance and cost efficiency. It involves diligent scrutiny to prevent resources from being over-provisioned, where too much capacity leads to wasteful spending on unused services, and underutilized, where insufficient resources can degrade performance and negatively impact the end-user experience.

- **Budget monitoring and reporting**: Budget monitoring and reporting are integral to the strategic deployment of cloud cost management tools, which equip organizations with instantaneous and granular insights into their cloud spending. This essential facet of cloud financial management plays a pivotal role in enabling businesses to navigate their cloud investments wisely. By providing a clear picture of current expenditures, these tools help organizations assess their resource allocation and utilization effectively, making it possible to identify areas of inefficiency and overspending. This proactive approach not only aids in circumventing budget overruns but also fosters a culture of financial accountability and optimization within the cloud environment.

- **Automatic cost controls**: Automating cost controls embodies a forward-thinking strategy for optimizing cloud expenditure, utilizing cutting-edge automation technologies to smartly regulate the consumption of cloud resources. This strategy involves the integration of scripts or sophisticated cloud management platforms capable of dynamically altering resource levels in response to real-time usage data. By automatically powering down inactive resources or decreasing the capacity of services during periods of diminished demand, this approach plays a pivotal role in curbing unnecessary spending. The essence of automating cost controls lies in its ability to guarantee that organizations are not wastefully allocating funds towards unused or minimally utilized resources, thereby ensuring operational expenditures are tightly aligned with actual needs.

With the introduction of RISE with SAP and GROW with SAP programs, SAP has streamlined the process of adopting and managing SAP environments for customers by bundling several critical components into a single offering. These components include SAP licensing fees, infrastructure hosting costs with providers like AWS, technical managed services costs for overseeing the SAP environment, and initial deployment costs. This consolidation aims to simplify budget planning for customers by reducing the number of separate items they need to account for in their financial planning. Essentially, SAP offers a more integrated and straightforward approach to deploying and managing SAP solutions, making it easier for customers to predict and manage their expenses related to SAP software, infrastructure, and services.

At the forefront of strategic IT transformation, customers are dedicating significant attention to the initial discovery and assessment phase of their current IT infrastructure. This critical first step serves as the cornerstone for meticulously planning the migration and modernization of their IT landscape. The essence of this phase lies in its ability to provide a comprehensive understanding of the existing system's architecture, pinpoint potential areas for enhancement, and develop a detailed strategic roadmap tailored for an effective transformation journey. As emphasized in earlier discussions, adopting core strategies such as maintaining a streamlined, 'clean core' by limiting customizations and proactively reducing technical debt is essential for optimizing costs throughout the planning process.

The concerted effort to mitigate technical debt is geared towards refining IT operations, encompassing actions like phasing out obsolete legacy systems, cutting down on superfluous licensing expenditures, and boosting the overall operational efficacy. Implementing these strategies not only leads to a nimbler and more responsive IT framework but also paves the way for more sophisticated cost management and optimization techniques. Such initiatives allow for the judicious allocation of resources, ensuring that investments are directed toward areas that promise the highest returns and contribute significantly to the organization's strategic objectives.

This comprehensive strategy towards modernizing the IT landscape emphasizes the significance of deliberate planning and the incorporation of industry best practices aimed at diminishing the operational and financial encumbrances linked to antiquated systems and inefficient methodologies. By adopting this holistic approach, organizations can anticipate not merely an upgrade in their technological base but a transformation in their operational ethos, leading to enhanced agility, improved efficiency, and a stronger alignment between IT expenditures and business value generation. This nuanced understanding and strategic execution in IT modernization underscore the critical role of thoughtful preparation and best practice adoption in overcoming the challenges posed by legacy constraints and operational inefficiencies, setting the stage for a future-ready, cost-optimized IT infrastructure.

Conclusion

In the ever-evolving IT landscape, balancing security and cost optimization remains a critical challenge, especially when integrating both SAP and non-SAP systems. As organizations navigate through business transformation and cloud migration journeys, the importance of security has reached unprecedented levels, becoming more crucial than ever before. Meanwhile, achieving cost predictability and optimization is essential for enabling businesses to allocate resources more strategically towards areas of differentiation and enhancement. This dual focus not only safeguards the integrity and resilience of the IT infrastructure but also empowers organizations to drive innovation and competitive advantage, ensuring that investments are directed toward initiatives that foster growth and value creation in the digital era.

Multiple choice questions

1. **What is the primary focus of the security paradigm for SAP applications in cloud environments?**

   a. Single-layer protection

   b. Network security only

   c. Multi-layered defense mechanisms

   d. Hardware protection

2. **In the shared responsibility model, what is typically the CSP's responsibility?**

   a. Application security

   b. Data security

   c. Infrastructure security

   d. User access management

3. **What is a key aspect of the SAP PrivateLink service?**

   a. Public internet access

   b. Private network connections

   c. Direct hardware access

   d. Manual routing

4. **What is a primary consideration in cost optimization for cloud deployments?**

   a. Maximum resource allocation

   b. Fixed infrastructure sizing

   c. Right-sizing of landscape

   d. Manual scaling only

5. **What type of VPN connection is supported in RISE with SAP?**

   a. Point-to-Site only

   b. Site-to-Site only

   c. Both Point-to-Site and Site-to-Site

   d. Neither type

6. **What is a key component of in-depth defense strategies?**

   a. Single security layer

   b. Multiple defensive measures

   c. Fixed security protocols

   d. Manual security checks

7. **What is the primary purpose of comprehensive data protection measures?**

   a. Network optimization

   b. Cost reduction

   c. Data security throughout the lifecycle

   d. Performance enhancement

8. **What type of connection is recommended for productive workloads?**

   a. Public internet

   b. Dedicated private connection

   c. Basic VPN

   d. Shared network

9. **What is a key aspect of budget monitoring and reporting?**

   a. Fixed cost allocation

   b. Manual tracking only

   c. Real-time cost insights

   d. Annual reviews

10. **What is the primary benefit of automatic cost controls?**

    a. Increased spending

    b. Manual resource management

    c. Dynamic resource optimization

    d. Fixed resource allocation

Answers

1. c

   Explanation: The security paradigm for SAP applications in cloud environments incorporates several layers of defense mechanisms to effectively counteract a wide spectrum of potential threats and vulnerabilities, ensuring comprehensive protection.

2. c

   Explanation: In the shared responsibility model, the CSP is responsible for protecting the cloud infrastructure, including the physical security of data centers, network systems, and core cloud software.

3. b

   Explanation: SAP PrivateLink enables secure access to cloud services through private network connections, bypassing the public internet and minimizing the risk of data exposure.

4. c

   Explanation: Right sizing of landscape is a critical aspect of cost optimization, ensuring resources are properly allocated based on actual needs and usage patterns.

5. b

   Explanation: RISE with SAP supports IPSec-based Site-to-Site (S2S) VPN connections over the Internet, while Point-to-Site (P2S) VPN scenarios are not supported.

6. b

   Explanation: In-depth defense strategies involve implementing multiple defensive measures at various levels within the system's architecture to create comprehensive protection against potential threats.

7. c

   Explanation: Comprehensive data protection measures aim to secure sensitive information across all stages of its lifecycle, including encryption at rest and in transit.

8. b

   Explanation: For accessing productive workloads, a dedicated private connection with redundancy is highly recommended to guarantee quality of service and higher availability levels.

9. c

   Explanation: Budget monitoring and reporting provide real-time and granular insights into cloud spending, enabling organizations to track and optimize their cloud investments effectively.

10. c

   Explanation: Automatic cost controls enable dynamic optimization of resource usage by automatically adjusting resource levels based on actual demand and usage patterns.

Join our book's Discord space

Join the book's Discord Workspace for Latest updates, Offers, Tech happenings around the world, New Release and Sessions with the Authors:

https://discord.bpbonline.com

CHAPTER 7
Concluding Remarks and Additional Resources

Introduction

The journey we have taken through SAP's technology landscape reveals a profound transformation in how enterprises operate, collaborate, and drive sustainable growth. Over the past year, we have witnessed unprecedented advancements in machine learning, generative AI, and purpose-built processors. However, perhaps more significantly, we have seen how these technological innovations converge to create something greater than the sum of their parts, a new paradigm for intelligent, sustainable enterprise operations.

Structure

The chapter covers the following topics:

- Dawn of integrated intelligence
- Financial dimension
- Next frontier of technology
- Convergence of generative AI and enterprise systems

- Convergence and innovation
- Future of work in the agentic enterprise

Objectives

This concluding chapter brings together the key themes and technologies we have explored throughout the book, offering a comprehensive perspective on the future of intelligent enterprises. As we wrap up our journey through SAP's technological landscape, you will gain a deeper understanding of how various components - from data intelligence to collaborative networks - work together to drive sustainable business transformation.

Through this chapter, you will see how organizations can measure and realize value across multiple dimensions, from operational excellence to sustainability. We will explore practical examples of how businesses are leveraging these integrated capabilities to create a lasting impact. This final discussion will help you connect the dots between different technologies and concepts covered in previous chapters, providing a clear vision of how enterprises can navigate their transformation journey in an increasingly complex business environment.

Dawn of integrated intelligence

At the heart of this transformation lies a powerful convergence of three critical elements: comprehensive data intelligence through SAP Business Data Cloud, collaborative business operations via SAP Business Network, and embedded sustainability practices that span entire value chains. This integration represents more than just technological advancement, it marks a fundamental shift in how organizations create and capture value.

Consider how a global manufacturer leverages this integrated approach. Their journey begins with SAP Business Data Cloud, where vast amounts of operational data are transformed into actionable insights through AI-powered analytics. These insights do not exist in isolation but flow seamlessly into their collaborative networks, where they inform decisions about everything from supplier selection to logistics optimization. All of this happens while maintaining a clear view of environmental impact, ensuring that efficiency and sustainability go hand in hand.

Evolution of enterprise data

The role of data in enterprise operations has undergone a remarkable evolution. No longer is data merely a byproduct of business operations; it has become the lifeblood of intelligent decision-making. SAP Business Data Cloud embodies this transformation by providing a unified platform where data maintains its critical business context across the entire enterprise landscape.

This preservation of context proves invaluable when organizations tackle complex challenges. Take the example of a consumer goods company wrestling with supply chain optimization. Through SAP Business Data Cloud, they can analyze historical demand patterns, current inventory levels, and supplier capacity, all within their proper business context. This contextual understanding enables them to make nuanced decisions that balance multiple objectives, from cost optimization to environmental impact.

Building trust through connection

The power of trusted data multiplies exponentially when combined with collaborative business networks. SAP Business Network, connecting over 5.5 million organizations globally, transforms how businesses interact and trade. This network effect creates a virtuous cycle where improved data quality leads to better collaboration, which in turn generates more reliable data.

A European automotive supplier illustrates this dynamic perfectly. By combining the analytical power of SAP Business Data Cloud with the collaborative capabilities of SAP Business Network, they have created a transparent, efficient supply chain that adapts in real-time to changing conditions. Their success relies not just on technology but on the trust built through verified partner credentials, transparent sustainability ratings, and shared digital twins for asset management.

Sustainable operations at scale

The integration of data intelligence and business networks creates unprecedented opportunities for scaling sustainable operations. Organizations can now track their environmental impact across entire value chains, from raw material sourcing to final product delivery. This visibility enables them to make informed decisions that balance economic and environmental considerations.

Consider how a global retailer uses this integrated approach to transform their logistics operations. By combining real-time data analytics with network collaboration, they have optimized their transportation routes to reduce carbon emissions while maintaining delivery efficiency. Their success demonstrates how sustainability and profitability can reinforce each other when supported by the right technological foundation.

Financial dimension

The transformation extends deeply into financial operations, where data-driven insights meet innovative financing models. Through the integration of SAP Business Data Cloud and SAP Business Network, organizations can now link financial incentives directly to sustainability performance. This creates a powerful mechanism for driving positive change throughout the value chain.

A multinational bank exemplifies this approach, using the platform to offer preferential financing terms to suppliers who meet specific sustainability criteria. The ability to verify environmental performance through trusted data makes this possible, creating a tangible link between sustainable practices and financial benefits.

Asset intelligence and optimization

The management of physical assets has been revolutionized through the combination of data intelligence and network collaboration. Digital twins, powered by real-time data and enhanced through collaborative insights, enable organizations to optimize asset performance while minimizing environmental impact.

Transformative innovation at work

The convergence of data intelligence and collaborative networks has fundamentally changed how organizations approach innovation. Rather than innovation occurring in isolated pockets, it now flows freely across organizational boundaries, powered by shared insights and collaborative experimentation. A pharmaceutical company demonstrates this transformation through their approach to drug development, where they leverage SAP Business Data Cloud's analytical capabilities to process vast amounts of research data while using SAP Business Network to coordinate with research partners globally.

This networked approach to innovation extends beyond product development into process improvement and sustainability initiatives. Manufacturing companies are discovering new ways to reduce waste and energy consumption by sharing best practices across the network while validating results through detailed data analysis. These innovations cascade through supply chains, creating multiplier effects that accelerate the transition to sustainable operations.

Power of collaborative ecosystems

The true potential of SAP's integrated approach becomes most apparent when examining how it enables ecosystem-wide collaboration. Take the example of a major automotive manufacturer that has transformed its entire supply chain into a dynamic, sustainability-focused ecosystem. Through SAP Business Network, they coordinate with hundreds of suppliers, each contributing data that flows into their SAP Business Data Cloud environment. This creates a comprehensive view of their operation's environmental impact, from raw material sourcing to final vehicle delivery.

The ecosystem approach proves particularly powerful when addressing complex sustainability challenges that no single organization can solve alone. A consortium of consumer goods companies demonstrates this by using the platform to collectively tackle plastic waste reduction. By sharing data about packaging materials, recycling processes, and consumer behavior, they are developing innovative solutions that benefit the entire industry.

Redefining industry standards

The integration of data intelligence and collaborative networks is redefining industry standards across sectors. In the chemical industry, companies are using SAP Business Data Cloud to track and analyze the environmental impact of their processes while leveraging SAP Business Network to coordinate with partners on developing greener alternatives. This combination of analytical power and collaborative capability enables them to accelerate the transition to sustainable chemistry while maintaining profitability.

Similar transformations are occurring in the retail sector, where companies are using integrated data and network capabilities to optimize their operations from source to shelf. A major retailer illustrates this by using real-time analytics to reduce food waste while coordinating with suppliers through the network to adjust ordering patterns dynamically. The result is a more sustainable operation that delivers both environmental and financial benefits.

Human element

Amid all these technological advancements, the human element remains crucial. Organizations succeeding with SAP's integrated solutions recognize that technology serves people, not the other way around. A global services company exemplifies this through its approach to digital transformation, where it uses SAP Business Data Cloud to provide employees with contextual insights that enhance decision-making while using SAP Business Network to facilitate collaboration with partners and clients.

The human dimension becomes particularly important when driving sustainability initiatives. Success requires not just the right technology but also cultural change and stakeholder engagement. Leading organizations use the platform to create transparency around their sustainability efforts, sharing progress and challenges with employees, partners, and customers to build trust and momentum for change.

Building future-ready organizations

The journey toward becoming a truly intelligent, sustainable enterprise requires organizations to build new capabilities while maintaining operational excellence. SAP's integrated approach provides the foundation for this transformation by enabling organizations to evolve at their own pace while keeping sight of their long-term objectives.

A global logistics company demonstrates this balanced approach to transformation. They began by using SAP Business Data Cloud to gain better visibility into their operations, then gradually expanded their use of SAP Business Network to coordinate more effectively with partners. As their capabilities matured, they introduced increasingly sophisticated sustainability initiatives, from optimizing routes to reduce emissions to coordinating with partners on shared environmental goals.

Art of implementation

The journey of digital transformation is as much about the path taken as the destination itself. Organizations that successfully implement SAP's integrated solutions understand that lasting change requires a thoughtful, measured approach. A global consumer products company illustrates this wisdom through its phased implementation strategy. They began by establishing a solid foundation with SAP Business Data Cloud, ensuring their data was trustworthy and contextually rich before expanding into advanced analytics and network collaboration.

Their journey started in the finance department, where they used SAP Business Data Cloud to create a single source of truth for financial reporting. As confidence in the data grew, they extended the platform's reach into supply chain operations, gradually integrating with SAP Business Network to enhance collaboration with suppliers. Each phase built upon the success of the previous one, creating momentum for change while managing risk.

Industry-specific pathways to success

While the fundamental principles of digital transformation remain consistent, the path to success varies significantly across industries. In healthcare, organizations focus on using SAP Business Data Cloud to analyze patient outcomes while leveraging SAP Business Network to coordinate with healthcare providers and suppliers. A leading hospital network demonstrates this approach by using integrated data analytics to optimize treatment protocols while collaborating with pharmaceutical companies to ensure reliable medical supply chains.

The manufacturing sector takes a different approach, emphasizing the integration of operational technology data with business systems. A precision engineering company shows how this works in practice, using SAP Business Data Cloud to analyze production data in real-time while coordinating with customers and suppliers through SAP Business Network to maintain optimal inventory levels and reduce waste.

Fostering adoption and change

The most sophisticated technology delivers value only when people embrace it. Successful organizations recognize that driving adoption requires a combination of clear communication, demonstrated value, and continuous support. A telecommunications company exemplifies this understanding through its approach to rolling out SAP's integrated solutions. They created a network of **digital champions** across the organization who could demonstrate the practical benefits of the new capabilities to their colleagues.

Their change management strategy went beyond traditional training to include collaborative learning sessions where teams could explore how the integrated capabilities of SAP Business Data Cloud and SAP Business Network could solve their specific challenges. This approach created organic momentum for adoption as people discovered new ways to enhance their work through the platform.

Optimizing resource utilization

The integration of data intelligence and collaborative networks creates unprecedented opportunities for resource optimization. A mining company demonstrates this potential through its comprehensive approach to asset management. Using SAP Business Data Cloud, they analyze equipment performance data to predict maintenance needs while leveraging SAP Business Network to coordinate with service providers and parts suppliers.

This integrated approach extends to human resource optimization as well. A professional services firm shows how combining workforce analytics from SAP Business Data Cloud with collaboration capabilities from SAP Business Network enables them to match talent with opportunities more effectively, improving both employee satisfaction and project outcomes.

Next frontier of technology

As technology continues to evolve, organizations must prepare for the integration of emerging capabilities. The combination of SAP Business Data Cloud and SAP Business Network provides a flexible foundation for incorporating new technologies as they mature. A technology manufacturer illustrates this adaptability through their approach to integrating quantum computing capabilities into their analytics framework while exploring blockchain applications for supply chain transparency.

The platform's open architecture ensures that organizations can experiment with new technologies without disrupting their core operations. An energy company demonstrates this by using the platform to pilot artificial intelligence applications for grid optimization while maintaining reliable operations through established processes.

Measuring impact and success

The true measure of digital transformation lies not in the technology implemented but in the value it creates. Organizations leading the way in this integrated approach understand that success must be measured across multiple dimensions. A global food and beverage company exemplifies this comprehensive approach to value measurement. Through SAP Business Data Cloud, they track traditional metrics like revenue and profitability alongside sustainability indicators such as carbon emissions and water usage. This holistic view enables them to demonstrate how sustainable practices drive business success.

Their measurement framework extends beyond internal metrics to capture ecosystem-wide impacts. Using SAP Business Network, they monitor supplier sustainability performance and collaborative innovation outcomes. This broader perspective helps them understand how their transformation efforts ripple through the value chain, creating multiplier effects that amplify the impact of their initiatives.

Power of partner ecosystems

Success in the digital age requires more than individual excellence, it demands effective collaboration across partner ecosystems. A leading automotive supplier demonstrates this through their approach to innovation. By combining the analytical capabilities of SAP Business Data Cloud with the collaborative features of SAP Business Network, they have created an innovation ecosystem that brings together suppliers, research institutions, and customers to accelerate the development of sustainable mobility solutions.

This ecosystem approach proves particularly powerful when addressing complex challenges that cross traditional industry boundaries. Consider how a consortium of chemical companies is working together to develop circular economy solutions. Through shared data analysis and collaborative experimentation, they are finding new ways to reduce waste and reuse materials, creating value while minimizing environmental impact.

Navigating regulatory complexity

As regulatory requirements around sustainability and data privacy continue to evolve, organizations need robust frameworks for ensuring compliance while maintaining operational agility. A multinational bank shows how the integration of SAP Business Data Cloud and SAP Business Network enables this balance. They use the platform's governance capabilities to enforce compliance requirements automatically while maintaining the flexibility to adapt to new regulations as they emerge.

Their approach extends beyond mere compliance to create a competitive advantage. By maintaining detailed audit trails and transparent reporting through the platform, they build trust with regulators and customers alike. This transparency proves particularly valuable in demonstrating their commitment to sustainable banking practices and responsible data management.

Realizing sustainable value

The journey toward becoming an intelligent, sustainable enterprise yields benefits that extend far beyond operational efficiency. A consumer goods manufacturer demonstrates how this integrated approach creates multiple forms of value. Through SAP Business Data Cloud, they have optimized their production processes to reduce energy consumption and waste. Meanwhile, the SAP Business Network enables them to collaborate with suppliers on sustainable packaging initiatives and circular economy programs.

The result is a virtuous cycle where sustainability initiatives drive business performance, which in turn enables further investment in sustainable practices. This company has reduced its carbon emissions by 30% while improving profit margins, proving that environmental and economic goals can reinforce each other when supported by the right technology platform.

Building future-ready teams

The success of digital transformation ultimately depends on the people who drive it forward. Organizations leading in this space recognize that building future-ready teams requires a combination of technical expertise and business acumen. A global logistics company illustrates this through its approach to talent development. They use SAP Business Data Cloud to analyze skill gaps and learning outcomes while leveraging SAP Business Network to connect employees with learning opportunities across their partner ecosystem.

Their talent development strategy emphasizes the importance of combining data literacy with sustainability awareness. Through hands-on experience with the platform, teams learn to use data-driven insights to drive sustainable business practices. This integrated approach to capability building ensures that technology investments translate into real business value.

Convergence of generative AI and enterprise systems

The emergence of **Large Language Models (LLMs)** and generative AI is fundamentally transforming how organizations interact with their enterprise systems. In the context of SAP's ecosystem, this transformation manifests in several concrete ways. Through SAP's GenAI Hub, organizations can now integrate LLMs directly into their business processes, creating new possibilities for automation, insight generation, and user interaction.

Consider how this integration is already reshaping core business processes. In procurement, LLMs analyze vast amounts of historical purchasing data through the SAP Business Network to identify optimal sourcing strategies while ensuring compliance with sustainability requirements. Natural language interfaces enable buyers to interact with complex procurement systems through conversational queries, receiving contextually relevant recommendations powered by both historical data and real-time market intelligence.

The impact extends deeply into financial operations, where generative AI assists in anomaly detection and reporting. Through SAP Business Data Cloud, LLMs analyze patterns in financial transactions, automatically flagging potential issues while generating narrative explanations that help finance teams understand the context and implications of their findings. This combination of analytical power and natural language generation transforms how organizations monitor and manage their financial health.

Practical applications and real-world impact

The integration of generative AI with ERP systems creates practical value across multiple dimensions.

In supply chain management, LLMs analyze unstructured data from supplier communications, market reports, and news feeds alongside structured operational data. This enables organizations to predict potential disruptions and automatically generate mitigation strategies. A manufacturing company demonstrates this capability by using AI-powered analysis to identify potential supply chain risks and automatically generate alternative sourcing strategies that maintain both operational efficiency and sustainability commitments.

Customer service sees a similar transformation through the integration of LLMs with SAP's Business Technology Platform. Service agents receive AI-generated summaries of customer interactions, complete with relevant context from ERP systems about order history, product specifications, and service entitlements. This integration enables more personalized service while reducing resolution times.

Future of work in AI-enhanced enterprise systems

Looking ahead, the convergence of generative AI and ERP systems will fundamentally change how people work with enterprise applications. The traditional interface between humans and systems is evolving from rigid form-based interactions to natural language conversations. SAP's Joule exemplifies this evolution, enabling users to interact with complex business systems through natural language while maintaining the precision and control required for enterprise operations.

These developments are particularly significant in the context of sustainability initiatives. Generative AI helps organizations understand and optimize their environmental impact by analyzing data across multiple systems and generating actionable insights. Through the SAP Business Network, these insights can be shared across partner ecosystems, creating collaborative opportunities for sustainability improvement.

Ensuring responsible AI in enterprise operations

The integration of generative AI into enterprise systems brings both opportunities and responsibilities. Organizations must ensure that AI systems maintain the same standards of accuracy, compliance, and ethical behavior that govern traditional business processes. SAP's approach to AI governance provides a framework for responsible AI deployment, ensuring that generative capabilities enhance rather than compromise business controls.

This governance extends to data quality and context preservation. Through SAP Business Data Cloud, organizations can ensure that AI systems have access to high-quality, contextually rich data while maintaining appropriate security and privacy controls. This foundation of trusted data is essential for realizing the full potential of generative AI in enterprise applications.

Convergence and innovation

The intersection of generative AI and ERP systems represents more than just technological advancement, it marks a fundamental shift in how organizations operate and create value. As these technologies mature, we can expect to see:

- Deeper integration between LLMs and business processes
- More sophisticated natural language interfaces for enterprise systems
- Enhanced predictive capabilities powered by AI analysis of business data
- Automated generation of business insights and recommendations
- New forms of collaboration enabled by AI-powered platforms

Dawn of the agentic enterprise

The convergence of generative AI and enterprise systems has given rise to a new paradigm: the agentic enterprise. At the forefront of this transformation are SAP Joule agents, representing a fundamental shift in how organizations leverage artificial intelligence. These agents, grounded in SAP's five decades of business process expertise, do more than just automate tasks; they collaborate, reason, and execute complex cross-functional processes with unprecedented sophistication.

Consider how this plays out in practice. A global manufacturing company deploys finance agents that work seamlessly with supply chain agents to optimize working capital. Through the SAP Knowledge Graph, these agents understand the full context of business operations, enabling them to make nuanced decisions that balance multiple objectives. When a supply chain disruption occurs, the agents do not just identify the problem; they collaborate to develop and implement solutions, drawing on their comprehensive understanding of business processes and access to real-time data through SAP Business Data Cloud.

Power of contextual intelligence

What sets SAP Joule agents apart is their deep grounding in a business context. Through integration with the SAP Knowledge Graph, these agents understand the intricate relationships between different business processes, data points, and organizational objectives. This contextual awareness enables them to tackle complex challenges that previously required extensive human intervention.

A financial services organization demonstrates the impact of this contextual intelligence. Their Joule agents analyze customer interaction data alongside financial transactions, regulatory requirements, and market conditions. This comprehensive view enables the agents to identify opportunities for process optimization while ensuring compliance with regulatory requirements. The agents do not just process information; they understand its business implications and act accordingly.

Collaborative intelligence at scale

The true power of SAP Joule agents emerges in their ability to work together, creating a network of specialized expertise that spans the enterprise. With access to over 1,300 prebuilt skills, these agents orchestrate complex business processes across SAP Business Suite and beyond. This collaborative capability transforms how organizations handle cross-functional challenges.

A retail company illustrates this transformation through its deployment of multiple specialized agents. Sales agents work in concert with inventory management agents and financial planning agents to optimize store operations. When a demand spike is detected, the agents collectively analyze the situation, adjust inventory levels, update financial forecasts, and modify staffing plans, all while maintaining alignment with the company's sustainability goals and budget constraints.

Democratizing AI through custom agent development

The introduction of the custom agent builder capability in SAP Build marks another significant step forward. This democratization of AI development enables organizations to create agents tailored to their specific needs without requiring deep technical expertise. Through a guided no-code workflow, business users can design agents that encapsulate their unique business logic and requirements.

A healthcare provider demonstrates the potential of custom agent development. Using SAP Build, they created specialized agents to handle patient scheduling, resource allocation, and inventory management. These custom agents work alongside standard SAP Joule agents, creating an integrated ecosystem that combines industry-specific knowledge with enterprise-wide process optimization.

Future of work in the agentic enterprise

As SAP Joule agents become more deeply integrated into business operations, we are seeing a fundamental shift in how people work. By 2024, these agents will support up to 80% of the most-used business tasks in SAP systems, transforming roles across finance, sales, human resources, and information technology. This is not about replacing human workers, it is about augmenting their capabilities and freeing them to focus on higher-value activities.

A professional services firm shows how this transformation enhances rather than replaces human expertise. Their consultants work alongside Joule agents who handle data analysis, report generation, and process optimization. The agents' ability to process vast amounts of information and identify patterns enables the consultants to develop more innovative solutions for their clients while ensuring consistent quality in service delivery.

Building the foundation for intelligent operations

The integration of SAP Joule agents across the enterprise requires a solid foundation of trusted data and robust processes. Through SAP Business Data Cloud, organizations ensure their agents have access to high-quality, contextually rich data that enables accurate decision-making. This integration creates a virtuous cycle where better data leads to more effective agent actions, which in turn generate more valuable data for future analysis.

Measuring success in the intelligent enterprise

The journey to becoming an intelligent, sustainable enterprise requires clear metrics to measure progress and validate outcomes. Through the integration of SAP Business Data Cloud and SAP Business Network, organizations can track both traditional performance indicators and emerging metrics that capture the full value of their digital transformation.

A global consumer products company illustrates this comprehensive approach to measurement. Through SAP Business Data Cloud, they track operational metrics that show immediate impact: a 30% reduction in processing time for financial closes, a 25% improvement in forecast accuracy, and a 40% reduction in manual data reconciliation efforts. Their Joule agents contribute to these improvements by automating routine tasks and providing predictive insights that enable proactive decision-making.

However, the metrics extend beyond operational efficiency. Through the SAP Business Network, they measure broader ecosystem impacts: a 22% reduction in supply chain emissions, a 15% improvement in supplier sustainability compliance, and a 35% faster onboarding of new trading partners. The combination of Joule agents and network collaboration has enabled them to achieve these results while maintaining profitability and growth.

Multi-dimensional nature of success

Success in the age of intelligent enterprises cannot be measured through traditional metrics alone. Organizations must track progress across multiple dimensions:

A pharmaceutical company demonstrates this through its balanced scorecard approach. They measure:

- **Operational excellence**: Through SAP Business Data Cloud, they track process automation rates, data quality metrics, and decision-making velocity. Their Joule agents have helped improve operational efficiency by 40% while reducing error rates by 65%.

- **Innovation impact**: The platform enables them to measure the speed of new product development, successful collaboration rates with research partners, and the impact of AI-driven insights on research outcomes.

- **Sustainability progress**: Using SAP Business Network, they monitor their environmental impact, supplier sustainability compliance, and progress toward circular economy goals.

- **Financial performance**: The integration of all these elements has resulted in a 28% improvement in working capital utilization and an 18% reduction in operational costs.

Conclusion

As we conclude our exploration of SAP's transformative technologies, it is clear that we stand at a pivotal moment in enterprise evolution. The convergence of trusted data through SAP Business Data Cloud, collaborative power through SAP Business Network, and intelligent automation through Joule agents creates unprecedented opportunities for organizations to reimagine their operations and impact.

The path forward requires organizations to think holistically about their transformation. Success comes not from implementing individual technologies but from creating an integrated ecosystem where data, networks, and AI work together to drive sustainable value creation. The organizations that thrive will be those that embrace this integrated approach while maintaining their focus on human-centered innovation and sustainable practices.

Your journey toward becoming an intelligent enterprise is unique, but you do not have to navigate it alone. Through SAP's comprehensive suite of solutions and the growing ecosystem of partners and collaborators, you have access to the tools, expertise, and support needed to succeed. Whether you are just beginning your transformation or looking to accelerate existing initiatives, the foundation for success is available today.

As you move forward, remember that transformation is not a destination but a continuous journey of innovation and improvement. The technologies and capabilities we have explored in this book provide the foundation for this journey, but your vision, commitment, and creativity will determine how far you can go.

We encourage you to take the next step in your transformation journey. Explore the resources available through SAP, engage with the community of innovators and practitioners, and begin building your roadmap to becoming an intelligent, sustainable enterprise. The future is not just something that happens to us, it is something we create together through the thoughtful application of technology in the service of human progress and planetary well-being.

Join our book's Discord space

Join the book's Discord Workspace for Latest updates, Offers, Tech happenings around the world, New Release and Sessions with the Authors:

https://discord.bpbonline.com

Index

W